UNTROUBLED

CONQUERING ANXIETY, FEAR & DEPRESSION

MILLER

MINISTRIES

Untroubled: Conquering Anxiety, Fear and Depression
ISBN: 978-0-9846918-5-2
Copyright © 2024 by Christine E. Miller

Published by:
Miller Ministries
4000 Westbrook Drive
Aurora, IL 60504 USA
(630) 851-4000
www.millerministries.org

Editor: Vincent M. Newfield | newfieldscreativeservices.com

Contents

Dedication

To all those who overcame opposition and then shared how to do the same, I will always cherish your teachings and the inspiration I've gleaned from them. I am particularly thankful for the wisdom and examples of Kenneth E. Hagin, and for my pastor, Nancy Dufresne, who brought truth in a simplified manner that helped me recognize some of my dysfunction and overcome it. I am also very grateful for my loving husband, Jeffrey, who continually encourages me to pursue the plan of God for my life. It is to him that I wish to dedicate this book.

Preface

I have written this book with one intention: to help set the captives free. Although I had the Bible and many great teachings to help me get delivered from anxiety, I could not find a resource available that was specifically geared toward this subject at the time I needed it. I believe a book like the one you are now holding provides the biblical and practical steps needed to navigate your way out of the pit of depression, panic, and anxiety and find freedom from fear in all its forms. May the Spirit of God speak to you through each chapter and use the truths presented to help you become all that Jesus died for you to be—completely whole in your soul.

SECTION 1
UNDERSTANDING THE ISSUE

Chapter 1

How Anxiety Began in My Life

"Therefore I [Jesus] tell you, stop being perpetually uneasy (anxious and worried) about your life…."

– Matthew 6:25 (AMPC)

Every person on this planet has been tempted to worry about or fear something in their life. Immediately after Adam and Eve disobeyed God in the Garden of Eden, fear entered the world. Since then, the whole world lies under the sway of Satan, and he will give you plenty of opportunities to worry and be afraid. I was no exception.

My life was filled with anxiety and worry from the time I was very young. I was unaware of the extent to which I worried about things in my life, until one day I had a wake-up call. I had put my children to bed and went to sit next to my husband to watch Christian television. As soon as I got still, I was suddenly hit with a panic attack. I'm not entirely sure why it happened when it did. I did not receive any bad news, and there wasn't anything out of the ordinary going on in my life. I'm sure I never had anything like this happen to me before, because I would have remembered it. It was the most horrible experience I've ever had from that day until this. Anybody who has ever had panic attacks could tell you they would have rather been diagnosed with a terminal illness than experience anxiety in that measure.

I got up and began to pace, and that did not help. I tried praying as hard and fast as I could, and that did not help. My husband offered a few suggestions, and I still did not improve. By morning, after a sleepless night, I knew I was in serious trouble. I was no better, and I could barely communicate with people at this point. I began to realize that if I was going to improve, I either needed to see a doctor, or get very serious about seeking God's help. Since the thought of seeing a doctor caused even more anxiety, I decided I would receive my complete healing by the Word and Spirit of God. I knew I could put my trust in a loving God more than I could in a physician.

I spent every waking moment reading and meditating upon the Word of God, confessing the Word, listening to scriptural messages, praying, and praising God. I began to gradually improve, and by the end of two weeks, I was completely free from the effects of that panic attack.

Through the process of seeking the Lord, I discovered I had been troubled by worry and fear my entire life. Just before having this panic attack, I had been worrying about some of our church members, about how I was raising my children, and about my age. However, I had not even realized I was worrying until I faced this crisis of anxiety. I was turning 30 that year, and for some reason, I got all worked up mentally about it. It seems so silly now in light of my current age. I made the decision after this never to worry about my age again, and I have not!

As with many people, my childhood circumstances were not perfect. My parents have always loved me and believed in me; I have known this ever since I was a child. However, they divorced when I was young. And as in many families, there was other dysfunction besides divorce. Because of all this, I took on a lot of responsibility at a young age; by the time I was a teenager I had become quite independent. I considered myself a strong person mentally and emotionally. Nevertheless, because of the unstable family conditions and the responsibilities I took on at a young age, I was actually worried and fearful most of the time. I wasn't really conscious of my anxiety, because I had learned to cope with it through strategies like staying very busy. I became an overachiever. But my unconscious coping mechanism merely masked the underlying anxiety. Worry was my constant companion, yet I didn't recognize what a problem it was. Not until years later did this anxiety surface in the form of a debilitating panic attack.

Don't Coddle or Cope with Fear

In my generation, fear was never coddled by parents, school teachers, or society, which in many ways was a healthier approach. The more attention you give to fear, the bigger it becomes. People today are more aware of anxiety and depression because of our school systems and social media. Although the stigma of having mental problems has been reduced, I believe there are also many more people who are crippled emotionally because they've been coddled, and their issues are given too much attention. In my situation, I had no choice but to press on with life in the presence of unrecognized fear.

Looking back, I see now that having this panic attack was a wake-up call. It helped me to realize I was worried and troubled about many things, and my journey to overcome this bad habit began. Since that time, I have also discovered that Satan will always try to come back to you with the thing you have been delivered from. I have learned to become aware of my thoughts and the strategies of the enemy, resisting the devil with the Word of God and the power of the Holy Spirit. I have now lived free from anxiety for many years. In this book, I am going to walk you through the steps you can take to enjoy the same victory in your life.

Be encouraged that whatever situation you are facing today, you can conquer anxiety and depression once and for all!

MY PRAYER CONFESSION OF FAITH:

Lord, thank You for speaking to me as I read through these pages. Open my spiritual eyes to see and understand Your nature and Your goodness more clearly. I believe I will receive complete freedom from fear, anxiety, and depression. In Your name, Jesus, Amen.

Chapter 2

What Are Anxiety and Depression?

"But understand this, that in the last days will come (set in) perilous times of great stress and trouble [hard to deal with and hard to bear]."

– 2 Timothy 3:1 (AMPC)

We are in it! We are living in times of great stress and trouble, hard to deal with and hard to bear. That is why there has been a dramatic increase in cases of anxiety and depression, as well as drug and alcohol use. According to the National Institute of Mental Health, more than one in five U.S. adults lives with a mental illness, which is nearly 60 million individuals.[1]

At the time of this writing, over 40 million adults in the U.S. have an anxiety disorder. One study showed that 31.9 percent of adolescents aged 13 to 18 are affected by an anxiety disorder.[2] These statistics reveal the severity of the mental problems that millions of people in our society are facing today.

I believe the greatest contributor to anxiety and depression is fear.

What Is Fear?

By definition, fear is "a painful emotion or passion excited by an expectation of evil, or the apprehension of impending danger."[3] Anxiety, worry, dread, and panic are all forms of fear. According to God's Word, fear is a spirit. In 2 Timothy 1:7, the apostle Paul tells us, *"For God has not given us a spirit of fear...."* The fact that fear is a spirit from the enemy is very important. It lets us know that it cannot be defeated with natural remedies. We must fight in the spirit and use spiritual weapons. While psychological methods and willpower can be helpful, spiritual issues must ultimately be dealt with spiritually to experience true freedom.

How Does Fear Come to Us?

Romans 10:17 says, *"So then faith comes by hearing, and hearing by the Word of God."* It's also important to know that fear comes by hearing negative information. With literally hundreds of channels to choose from 24 hours a day, and a constant feed of news and social media, people are hearing and hearing more information on a daily basis than ever before in human history. More than 2,500 years ago, the prophet Daniel prophesied about our day, saying: *"But you Daniel, keep this prophecy a secret; seal up the book until the time of the end, when many will rush here and there, and knowledge will increase"* (Daniel 12:4, NLT).

Without question, knowledge has increased and continues to do so at a rapid pace. Studies show that prior to 1900 AD, knowledge appeared to be doubling every 100 years. By the end of WWII, knowledge was doubling every 25 years. Today, it is estimated that human knowledge is doubling every 13 months.[4] Unfortunately, most of the information we hear daily is unprofitable and fuels the fire of fear and anxiety.

Considering the enormous influence of what we are taking in, it is easy to see why God says, *"Guard your heart above all else...."*(Proverbs 4:23, NLT), and *"Do not conform to the pattern of this world, but be transformed by the renewing of your mind...."* (Romans 12:2, NIV).

Your heart and mind are inseparably connected. When you guard—or attentively keep watch—over what you are allowing your ears to hear and your eyes to see, you can prevent fear from entering your life. And when you renew your mind by reading and meditating on God's Word, you are deleting the wrong information and replacing it with the right information.

What About Anxiety and Depression?

The terms anxiety and depression are used so often in our day, and sometimes in the wrong context. I believe it would be helpful to define anxiety and depression.

According to Noah Webster's original dictionary, anxiety is defined as "concern or worry respecting some event, future or uncertain, which disturbs the mind, and keeps it in a state of painful uneasiness."[5] This anxiety usually springs from fear or serious apprehension of evil.

In today's world, there is a condition referred to as generalized anxiety disorder (GAD). This is a persistent feeling of anxiety or dread, which can interfere with daily life according to the National Institute of Mental Health.[6] Rather than just being temporarily worried or fearful about something, individuals with an anxiety disorder live in a state of perpetual mental uneasiness. Symptoms include feeling restless, on edge, and easily fatigued, along with a difficulty concentrating, irritableness, headaches, stomach aches, and problems sleeping.

Again, as I've already noted, the scriptural definition of anxiety is simply fear. Worry is like an identical twin to anxiety, and it is also a form of fear. Studies show that if a person continues in a habit of worrying long enough, it will actually wear down the good chemicals in their brain, like serotonin, that help us maintain a healthy mental state.

Anxiety and depression can actually go hand-in-hand. Researchers at the Mayo Clinic describe depression as "a mood disorder that produces a persistent feeling of sadness and loss of interest, and it affects how one feels, thinks, and handles daily activities."[7] The symptoms are virtually the same as those of anxiety, with the added feelings of guilt, worthlessness, emptiness, hopelessness, and sometimes thoughts of death or suicide. It is also not uncommon for those dealing with depression to have a lack of energy or angry outbursts over seemingly insignificant issues.

What Is the Cure for These Disorders?

Although medical science can help with therapy and various medications, they are not cures for these disorders. While a doctor's prescription can certainly help alleviate several of these symptoms, many people report that their medications start losing their effectiveness after a period of time.

Some mental illnesses are caused by a chemical imbalance, and some are induced by a negative situation. We also know from the Word of God that some of these disorders are actually caused by an evil spirit. In such cases, there is not a medication or therapy on earth that can drive an evil spirit out of a person.

Keep in mind that Satan is the god of this world system, and he only has despair to offer people. Second Corinthians 4:4 from the Amplified Classic translation says, *"For the god of this world has blinded the unbelievers' minds [that they should not discern the truth], preventing them from seeing the illuminating light of the Gospel of the glory of Christ (the Messiah), Who is the Image and Likeness of God."*

If I just left you with this information, you could certainly feel anxious or depressed about life. But if you have made Jesus the Lord and Savior of your life, you are no longer under Satan's control. And the great news is that for the believer who is acting upon the Word of God, you can experience complete freedom from these disorders!

God has given us answers in Scripture that actually work if we will be diligent to do them. The Bible says *"Anxiety in the heart of man causes depression, but a good word makes it glad"* (Proverbs 12:25).

Although my life was once imprisoned by anxiety and worry, I received freedom when I began speaking and acting on the principles of God's Word. He is not a respecter of persons. What He did for me He will do for you as you faithfully stand on and live by His Word.

MY PRAYER CONFESSION OF FAITH:

Lord, I desire to live completely free from every mental and emotional disorder. Help me to guard my heart and mind daily, being mindful to recognize and keep out what is bad but purposely take in what is good. I want to know and live Your Word, and as I continue to read and study it—and go through the chapters of this book—I believe I will receive the answers I need to experience all the freedom You paid for. In Your name, Jesus, Amen.

---

[1] Mental Illness (https://www.nimh.nih.gov/health/statistics/mental-illness; accessed 4/18/24).

[2] Anxiety Statistics and Facts (https://www.forbes.com/health/mind/anxiety-statistics/; accessed 6/21/24).

[3] American Dictionary of the English Language, Noah Webster 1828 (San Francisco, CA: Foundation for American Christian Education, 1967, 1995).

[4] "Knowledge Doubling Every 12 Months, Soon to be Every 12 Hours" David Russell Schilling (https://www.industrytap.com/knowledge-doubling-every-12-months-soon-to-be-every-12-hours/3950; accessed 4/18/24).

[5] Definition of anxiety, see note 5.

[6] Generalized Anxiety Disorder (https://www.nimh.nih.gov/health/trials/generalized-anxiety-disorder; accessed 6/21/24).

[7] Depression (major depressive disorder) (https://www.mayoclinic.org/diseases-conditions/depression/symptoms-causes/syc-20356007; accessed 6/21/24).

SECTION 2

WHAT BELONGS TO YOU
THROUGH CHRIST

Chapter 3

Our Inheritance of Peace

"But He was wounded for our transgressions, He was bruised for our guilt and iniquities; the chastisement [needful to obtain] peace and well-being for us was upon Him, and with the stripes [that wounded] Him we are healed and made whole."

– Isaiah 53:5 (AMPC)

Peace is everything. If you don't have peace, you cannot enjoy life. It doesn't matter how big and beautiful your house is, how fancy the car you drive, how prestigious your job is, or how much money you have saved. Without peace in your heart and mind, nothing is satisfying.

The prophet Isaiah tells us that one of the reasons Jesus came was to give us peace. To provide us with such a priceless treasure, Christ had to first take the punishment for our sins, which is death. Yes, sin started with Adam. But God's Word says, *"For all have sinned and fall short of the glory of God,"* and *"the wages of sin is death...."* (Romans 3:23; 6:23). Make no mistake: for us to obtain peace and well-being, it was necessary for Jesus to be chastised (or punished) in our place, thereby becoming our substitute.

Through His death on the cross, God's justice was met, and our sin debt was paid. When Christ rose from the dead, our total redemption was accomplished, and through Him, we now have peace. It is a done deal. When we place our faith in Jesus, we have the same peace that God has! It is a major part of our inheritance in Him.

There Are Two Kinds of Peace

Just before going to the cross, Jesus spent the final hours of His life downloading a great deal of wisdom and truth into His disciples. The apostle John documents His final words, including this very powerful statement, which is recorded in John 14:27: *"Peace I leave with you, My peace I give to you; not as the world gives do I give to you. Let not your heart be troubled, neither let it be afraid."*

According to this verse, there are two types of peace. There is peace that Jesus gives, and there is peace that the world gives.

The peace the world offers is a feeling of security based on agreeable circumstances. It is an outward, external peace. As long as you don't have any sickness or pain in your body, you have plenty of money, your relationships are doing well, and there are no conflicts at work or with your family and friends, you are at peace.

The problem with this peace the world offers is that it is fragile and fleeting. As soon as a circumstance takes a downward, negative turn, this peace is gone. In its place, anxiety and worry rush in to fill the void.

The world doesn't have any lasting peace to offer you. Satan, the god of this world, only offers an illusion of peace. It is a false expectation or false hope that will always leave you with disappointment. Jesus called Satan the thief, telling us, *"The thief cometh not, but for to steal, and to kill, and to destroy: I am come that they might have life, and that they might have it more abundantly"* (John 10:10, KJV).

If you want true, lasting peace, you won't find it in this world, which is under Satan's control. Apart from Jesus, Satan will steal, kill, and destroy anything good in your life. Thank God there is another kind of peace available to you if you are born again. It is the peace of Jesus.

The peace Jesus offers will keep you calm and content regardless of the circumstances! His peace is unshakable and constant forever because He is peace. The Bible says, *"For He is [Himself] our peace...."* (Ephesians 2:14, AMPC).

Therefore, when Jesus said, *"Peace I leave with you, My peace I give to you...."*, He was giving us Himself. Indeed, He is the Prince of Peace who has taken up permanent residence inside us in the form of His Spirit. If you have received salvation through Jesus, you have His peace because you have Him!

"If I Have the Peace of God, Why Do I Feel So Troubled?"

Many Christians ask this question. You may be asking it too. The reason so many believers are not experiencing God's peace is because the enemy has stolen their peace by manipulating their emotions.

The fact is you will feel many different types of emotions throughout your lifetime, and your feelings are attached to your thoughts. Satan's primary target is the mind. His strategy is to suggest a troubling thought to you and accompany that thought with a feeling, which makes it seem real.

For example, he may inject a thought into your mind that says, *I'm worthless*, and with that thought, he will attach a sinking feeling of condemnation and guilt, and even bring up memories of past failures. If you don't know the truth of who you are in Christ, you will unknowingly swallow Satan's lie and surrender your peace.

That is why it is vital for you to know God's Word. His Word is truth, and it never changes. When you know the truth, you can recognize and reject Satan's lies and learn how to "cast down" every ungodly thought and imagination that comes into your mind—regardless of how convincing or real it feels.

Peace Is Wholeness in Every Area of Life

In the Old Testament, the primary word for peace is the Hebrew word *shalom*, which conveys the idea of wholeness in every area of one's life. This word is so special and sacred to Jews that it is used as a greeting when meeting and departing from a loved one. To say "shalom" to someone is to speak a blessing of safety, welfare, health, peace, rest, and prosperity over their life.

Unfortunately, many people today have plenty of money, but they do not have true peace. That is, they lack wholeness in areas like their relationships as well as their health. God states clearly in His Word, *"Beloved, I pray that you may prosper in all things and be in health, just as your soul prospers"* (3 John 2). Mentally, emotionally, physically, and spiritually, God wants you to prosper and experience His peace.

You Are a Three-Part Being

1 THESSALONIANS 5:23
Now may the God of peace Himself sanctify you completely; and may your whole spirit, soul, and body be preserved blameless at the coming of our Lord Jesus Christ.

The peace that Jesus offers is complete and it is meant to permeate and preserve every aspect of who we are. Each of us is a three-part being, created in the image of God. We are a spirit, we have a soul, and we live in a physical body. To successfully live in victory, every believer must understand the difference between the three.

The spirit is the innermost part of who you are. The moment you invite Jesus to be your Lord and Savior, your spirit is "born again"! You become a "new creation" in Christ (see 1 Corinthians 5:7).

The soul consists of your mind, will, and emotions. It is the part of you that thinks, feels, and makes decisions. Unlike your spirit, which is instantly transformed, your soul is continually being transformed throughout your lifetime. This is done by renewing your mind with the Word of God.

The body is the physical part of you that your spirit and soul live in while on this earth. As a believer in Christ, *"…your body is the temple of the Holy Spirit, who lives in you and was given to you by God…."* (1 Corinthians 6:19, NLT).

The Mind of the Flesh vs. the Mind of the Spirit

God's Word says that before we came to Christ, we were spiritually dead in our sins, dominated by the devil, and under the control of our fleshly desires (see Ephesians 2:1-3). The moment we were born again, God's Spirit made a permanent home in our spirit, resurrecting our spirit man and enabling it to take the leadership role over our soul and body. A born again spirit will always side with God's Word and God's Spirit and take us in the right direction.

Our flesh, however, has not been made new yet. The Bible says that our flesh—which is the combination of our unrenewed soul and body—is against God. In fact, Romans 8:7 (AMPC) tells us, *"...The mind of the flesh [with its carnal thoughts and purposes] is hostile to God, for it does not submit itself to God's Law; indeed it cannot."*

Your flesh will take you straight to hell if you let it. How severe are the consequences of following your flesh? Again, we turn to the words of Paul:

> **ROMANS 8:6 (AMPC)**
> **Now the mind of the flesh [which is sense and reason without the Holy Spirit] is death [death that comprises all the miseries arising from sin, both here and hereafter]. But the mind of the [Holy] Spirit is life and [soul] peace [both now and forever].**

Your soul is the deciding factor on how you respond to circumstances and temptations. If you live listening to and obeying the mind of your flesh, you will live a miserable life. However, if you choose to renew your mind with the Word of God, taking time to read and study it daily, you will gain the spiritual strength needed to listen to and obey the mind of the Spirit. The results will be *"...life and [soul] peace [both now and forever]"* (Romans 8:6, AMPC).

Your renewed mind will recognize and reject ungodly thoughts, like that thought of worthlessness we talked about earlier. The idea that you are worthless is a lie that goes against God's Word. The Bible teaches us that we are so valuable that Jesus gave His precious blood to pay for our sins and purchase us out of Satan's dominion (see 1 Peter 1:18-19).

Once your renewed mind recognizes Satan's lies, you must choose to reject his thoughts and override any feelings that accompany them. Then speak the truth over your life and against the enemy.

The Word Peace Carries the Idea of Oneness

What is interesting is that in the New Testament, one of the meanings for the word *peace* is "quietness, oneness, or to set at one again." To be one means having one thought, not many, and not being double-minded. A troubled mind will race in multiple directions with many different thoughts and emotions.

People who experience anxiety have numerous thoughts bombarding their minds, sometimes like the rapid fire of a machine gun. When this barrage of thoughts comes, it causes confusion, panic, and uncertainty. As the mental and emotional negativity snowballs, assurance in God's ability decreases, and one begins to think and say, *Oh my God! What am I going to do?*

If you find yourself in that condition, don't trust your own judgment. Instead, search God's Word for Scriptures that pertain to what you're panicking about and begin to mentally chew on those verses. As you turn them over in your mind and speak them out loud, the negative thoughts will be silenced and singleness (or oneness) of thought will be restored.

When you are single-minded, you are trusting and resting in what God says in His Word about you and your situation. You are not considering what you see, how you feel, or what the enemy or anyone else is trying to tell you. As a result, the peace of God will set your mind in quietness again, because His peace accompanies His Word, which is His thoughts and feelings.

I love what the Bible says in 1 Corinthians 2:16 (AMPC). It declares that *"...we have the mind of Christ (the Messiah) and do hold the thoughts (feelings and purposes) of His heart."* The peace of God is so powerful it is able to keep us calm as we pray and surrender our anxiety to Him. This is what Peter admonished when he said,

1 PETER 5:7 (AMPC)
Casting the whole of your care [all your anxieties, all your worries, all your concerns, once and for all] on Him, for He cares for you affectionately and cares about you watchfully.

Trusting that what God says is true will bring you into His peace. Remember, *"God is not a man, so he does not lie. He is not human, so he does not change his mind. Has he ever spoken and failed to act? Has he ever promised and not carried it through?"* (Numbers 23:19, NLT). The more you believe that God cannot lie, the greater the assurance and peace His Word will bring.

When You Stay in Peace,
You Stay in Control in Difficult Situations

Without question, God's peace is a powerful force. That is why the devil is always trying to steal it. Your power to overcome anything in life is rooted in maintaining a calm, peaceful, and trusting attitude. When you give place to anxious, fearful thoughts in your mind, you allow the devil to take the driver's seat. But when you choose to trust God's Word and live in His peace, you give His Spirit—who is living in your spirit—charge of your life.

People who stay in peace stay in control and handle situations successfully. Jesus gives us a vivid picture of what this looks like when He and His disciples crossed the sea of Galilee during a major storm. Here is what happened, according to Mark's gospel:

MARK 4:35-38 (KJV)
35 And the same day, when the even was come, he saith unto them, Let us pass over unto the other side.
36 And when they had sent away the multitude, they took him even as he was in the ship. And there were also with him other little ships.
37 And there arose a great storm of wind, and the waves beat into the ship, so that it was now full.
38 And he was in the hinder part of the ship, asleep on a pillow....

Now, many of Jesus' disciples were seasoned fishermen who knew how to deal with storms. So why did they panic and become so terrified by this storm? The Amplified Classic translation shines a light on the reason, telling us it was *"...a furious storm of wind [of hurricane proportions]..."* (Mark 4:37, AMPC). Thus, the intensity of this tempest was likely beyond what they had previously experienced.

Yet, right in the middle of the storm, the Bible says that Jesus slept. He had already given the faith command to go to the other side of the lake. He had received this direction from the Father. Therefore, He knew He would arrive safely because He believed in His Father's word. This trust in God's word gave Jesus singleness of mind that resulted in peace. He knew in His heart that the Father would do what He said, and they would arrive safely on the other side.

But when the disciples experienced the storm of hurricane proportions, they weren't so sure, and they began to panic.

> **MARK 4:38-41 (KJV)**
> **38 ...And they awake him, and say unto him, Master, carest thou not that we perish?**
> **39 And he arose, and rebuked the wind, and said unto the sea, Peace, be still. And the wind ceased, and there was a great calm.**
> **40 And he said unto them, Why are ye so fearful? how is it that ye have no faith?**
> **41 And they feared exceedingly, and said one to another, What manner of man is this, that even the wind and the sea obey him?**

Now there's an important point in this passage I don't want you to miss. When the disciples asked, "What manner of man is this, that even the wind and sea obey him?" many readers simply answer, "Well, naturally, He is the Son of God!" But I believe the real point being made is that this type of man—the man who operates in the peace and assurance of God's Word—is powerful and is in control of his circumstances.

From our vantage point, we could easily become critical of the disciples for the way they acted. But before we do, let's stop and think of how many times we have thought or even asked the Lord, "Don't You care that I'm going through this difficult time? Don't You hear me crying out to You for help? Can't You do something to change this situation?" The truth is there is absolutely no faith in those types of questions.

Of course God cares! He is simply waiting for you to trust Him and yield to His peace so His power can flow into your situation and change it. During the fierce storm, Jesus trusted the Father's guidance and remained in peace. This put Him in the driver's seat. He used the same supernatural authority and power that is available to us and calmed the wind and the waves. Jesus and the disciples then made it safely to the other side of the lake just as He had said.

Another important attribute of the peace of Jesus is that you never read anywhere in the gospels where He was in a rush. Even when Lazarus, His close friend, had died, He waited two more days before going to see Lazarus to raise him back to life. Not even the tragic circumstances of losing a loved one could drive Jesus into giving up His peace.

Let Christ's Peace Lead the Way

Anxiety, worry, and panic all have a driving nature. That is how the devil, the world, and your flesh operate. The types of thoughts and feelings they bring put extreme pressure on you and drive you to make faulty decisions.

In contrast, the nature of the Holy Spirit is gentle and peaceful. When He is leading and guiding you, He will often do so by softly nudging you to go a certain way. Isaiah 55:12 says, *"For you shall go out with joy, and be led out with peace...."*

It is important to see that God will never lead you or direct you through feelings of anxiety, worry, or fear. Many have been afraid of making a mistake in an area of their life and have become anxious or felt pressured to make a decision. If you are feeling anxious or pressured, don't make any decisions. Be still and know that God will never guide you in that way.

Simply wait and watch for His leading. If He is directing you, you will have an inner peace like a green light giving you the go ahead. In every decision, let Christ's peace lead the way.

COLOSSIANS 3:15 (AMPC)
And let the peace (soul harmony which comes) from Christ rule (act as umpire continually) in your hearts [deciding and settling with finality all questions that arise in your minds, in that peaceful state] to which as [members of Christ's] one body you were also called [to live]. And be thankful (appreciative), [giving praise to God always].

MY PRAYER CONFESSION OF FAITH:

Lord, help me to trust Your Word over the fearful things I see, feel, and think. Like You, Jesus, help me to stay in peace and appropriate Your power by right thinking and right speaking. No longer will I follow the mind of my flesh; from now on I choose to follow the mind of the Holy Spirit. I want Your peace to rule like an umpire in my heart in every decision, deciding and settling with finality all questions that arise in my mind. In Your name, Jesus, Amen.

Chapter 4

Thought Control

"For the weapons of our warfare are not carnal but mighty in God for pulling down strongholds, casting down arguments and every high thing that exalts itself against the knowledge of God, bringing every thought into captivity to the obedience of Christ."

– 2 Corinthians 10:4-5

To effectively live free from anxiety and depression, you must learn how to take control of your thoughts. This practice starts with and is maintained by knowing God's Word and feeding on it daily. The more we know the truth of the Word, the more we can recognize and reject the enemy's lies. In this chapter, we will see how Satan seeks to build strongholds in our mind through thoughts of temptation and doubts about God's Word. Doubt can be the door to unbelief, and keep us from inheriting the promises of God.

Thankfully, God has given us powerful spiritual weapons to destroy strongholds of ungodly thinking. We can take captive every thought and imagination that attempts to exalt itself above the truth of God's Word. With His help we can learn to let truth triumph over the enemy's lies and escape the trap of becoming double-minded.

What Does It Mean to Be Double-Minded?

In our last chapter, we learned that one of the meanings of the word *peace* is oneness or to set at one again. It is the idea of being single-minded and having our focus on one thing—the truth of God's Word.

The opposite of being single-minded is being double-minded. This describes a person who keeps switching back and forth between two differing lines of thinking. James, the half-brother of Jesus, talks about this in the first few verses of his New Testament letter.

> **JAMES 1:5-8**
> **5   If any of you lacks wisdom, let him ask of God, who gives to all liberally and without reproach, and it will be given to him.**
> **6   But let him ask in faith, with no doubting, for he who doubts is like a wave of the sea driven and tossed by the wind.**
> **7   For let not that man suppose that he will receive anything from the Lord;**
> **8   He is a double-minded man, unstable in all his ways.**

The Amplified Classic translation defines *double-mindedness* as *"...a man of two minds (hesitating, dubious, irresolute), [he is] unstable and unreliable and uncertain about everything [he thinks, feels, decides]"* (James 1:8). Clearly, a person who is double-minded is a person without peace. No one can think and believe what God's Word says and simultaneously hold on to thoughts that are contradictory to the Word and expect to experience what the Word promises. Double-mindedness will only produce confusion, chaos, and instability.

On the other hand, when we are single-minded, trusting in God's Word, we have His peace and are in faith. Where there is no hesitating and no doubting, God's Word will surely come to pass. Thus, the goal of every believer should be to have a single mind that knows and holds fast to the Word. This can only happen if we are diligent to control our thoughts.

The Devil's Wants You Double-Minded

Now Satan knows that if we are double-minded, we will lack God's peace and fail to see His promises come to pass. That is why he is always working his plan to gain access to our mind and take charge of our thinking. This is exactly what we see taking place in Genesis 3 when Satan entered Eden and deceived Eve. His first recorded activity in Scripture was to deceive Eve into being double-minded about the word God had spoken.

GENESIS 3:1-5
1 Now the serpent was more cunning than any beast of the field which the Lord God had made.

> And he said to the woman, "Has God indeed said,
> 'You shall not eat of every tree of the garden'?"
> 2   And the woman said to the serpent, "We may
> eat the fruit of the trees of the garden;
> 3   But of the fruit of the tree which is in the
> midst of the garden, God has said, 'You shall not
> eat it, nor shall you touch it, lest you die.'"
> 4   Then the serpent said to the woman, "You
> will not surely die.
> 5   For God knows that in the day you eat of it
> your eyes will be opened, and you will be like
> God, knowing good and evil."

Eve started out single-minded, believing and quoting the word of God to the serpent. But the serpent interjected an opposite thought, causing Eve to question the integrity of what God said. She was enticed to believe another thought about her circumstance. At face value, it seemed harmless. However, that seemingly harmless thought moved her and Adam to rebel against God, and their disobedience catapulted all of mankind into a broken, fallen state.

If you think about it, every sinful act begins with a subtle, seemingly harmless thought, which is interwoven with doubt about something God said. If you doubt God's Word, you will not enjoy God's peace, because His Word is the assurance we need to remain stable and in peace, especially in times of trouble.

In Eve's case, once Satan whispered that she would "not surely die" and that her eyes would be opened and she would be like God, multiple doubts began swirling in her head about what God said. *Is it necessary to stay away from the tree of the knowledge of good and evil?* she thought. *Is this fruit really bad, and are we really going to die? Is God trying to keep something from us? Will the fruit make us as wise as Him, and He doesn't want that?*

You know what happened. Eve swallowed the lie, ate the forbidden fruit, and got Adam to join her. Giving in to the devil's doubt got them thrown out of the garden. Sin and death entered humanity and the world, and we are still dealing with the repercussions of their disobedience. This is one of the reasons why this book is needed today.

If You Give the Enemy an Inch, He'll Take Ten Miles

The thoughts Satan brings will always downplay the seriousness of a sinful action. He will drop ideas in your mind like:

Go ahead and lie to protect your reputation. You need to keep your job.

It's okay to dream about someone else's spouse; you're not hurting anyone.

Never forget what that person did to you. Keep a record of it and make them pay for it.

Sure, God delivered you in the past. But will He deliver you this time?

Or maybe you've heard the enemy whisper, *Just this one time won't hurt anything.* The truth is, if you give yourself the liberty of indulging your mind once, the thought will come back stronger the second time. Every time you accept rather than reject the devil's deceptions and doubts, each successive thought on the subject will become stronger and stronger. That is how strongholds are built in the mind.

Before you know it, you are in bondage to wrong thinking, which will ultimately lead to wrong speaking and wrong actions if left unchecked. For example, no one ever committed adultery without first turning the thought over and over in their mind for a season.

Indulging the mind will always lead to indulging the flesh.

Little by little, the devil weaves his tapestry of lies with the purpose of trying to get us to the place where we doubt the seriousness of our actions and think there will be no consequences for our sin. In that moment, the hook of his deception is set, and we are caught in his clutches. Here's how the Bible describes the temptation-to-sin scenario:

> **JAMES 1:14-15**
> **14 But each one is tempted when he is drawn away by his own desires and enticed.**
> **15 Then, when desire has conceived, it gives birth to sin; and sin, when it is full-grown, brings forth death.**

Make no mistake: Satan's intended end for all who sin is death. Regardless of the sin, the same subtle scenario is set into motion. The enemy tempts us with thoughts and feelings that ignite a fire of ungodly desire in us. And this is not just with the enticement to commit adultery. This principle applies to issues of panic and depression. No one ever had a panic attack without first entertaining wrong thoughts repeatedly. No one ever fell into depression without first entertaining negative lies. Anxiety and depression come from doubt, and doubt opens the door to unbelief, which is sin.

The children of Israel could not enter the Promised Land because of unbelief. God's Word says, *"...They were not able to enter [into His rest], because of their unwillingness to adhere to and trust in and rely on God [unbelief had shut them out]"* (Hebrews 3:19, AMPC). If you find yourself battling with anxiety or depression, doubt and unbelief are at the root of it. Doubt opens the door to the devil's trap of double-mindedness. The way to avoid this trap is by learning to control your thought life.

It's Always a Matter of Trust

Although we may not want to admit it, all of us are tempted to be double-minded. I remember a time when our ministry was under a difficult spiritual and financial attack. My husband and I had been praying and standing on the Word of God for a breakthrough, but after a period of several months, things had hardly changed.

I had been working full time for the church we pastor, but since I was a registered nurse, I decided to look for a job in the medical profession. One day while praying, I had an unusual spiritual encounter with the Lord. Unexpectedly, I was wrapped in His presence in a way that has rarely happened to me. He led me to read John 21 and asked me, just like He asked Peter, if I loved Him. When I responded, "You know I love You, Lord," He said, "Feed My sheep."

That encounter let me know that getting a job as a nurse would profit me nothing! I had become double-minded and anxious concerning God's provision because of our negative circumstances. This is the same thing that happened to Peter. With Jesus gone, he became concerned about his livelihood. So, he decided to go fishing, and in the process, he ended up leading some of the other apostles astray with him. After toiling all night long, he caught nothing. But when Jesus showed up, they caught a boatload of fish.

Jesus wanted Peter to give himself to full-time ministry and to trust Him for his provision. That is also what the Lord wanted me to do, and He wants you to trust Him as well. With every challenge we face, it always comes down to the issue of trust. Whether the struggle is financial, relational, or an issue of health, God will use it to help us see what we are truly trusting—Him or our own abilities and resources.

Because of the words that Jesus spoke to me during my prayer time, I was able to refocus on His faithfulness. I became single-minded once again, knowing He would provide for us. My trust in Him was restored, and within a short time, the finances began to come in again. Once more, God proved Himself to be faithful!

Satan Seeks to Build Strongholds

The number one need of every believer is to renew the mind. Remember, you are a three-part being—spirit, soul, and body. The moment you receive Jesus as your Lord and Savior, your spirit is instantly changed into a new creation. The Bible teaches, *"...The old [previous moral and spiritual condition] has passed away. Behold, the fresh and new has come!"* (2 Corinthians 5:17, AMPC)

Satan can no longer tamper with your spirit. His mode of attack is against your mind, which is a part of your soul. Again and again, he injects one wrong thought after another. His aim, as I already mentioned, is to get you to accept his doubts and deceptions so that he can build strongholds of wrong thinking in your mind.

The apostle Paul understood the dynamics of our spiritual battle and wrote this about it:

> **2 CORINTHIANS 10:3-5 (AMPC)**
> **3 For though we walk (live) in the flesh, we are not carrying on our warfare according to the flesh and using mere human weapons.**
> **4 For the weapons of our warfare are not physical [weapons of flesh and blood], but they are mighty before God for the overthrow and destruction of strongholds,**
> **5 [Inasmuch as we] refute arguments and theories and reasonings and every proud and lofty thing that sets itself up against the [true] knowledge of God; and we lead every thought and purpose away captive into the obedience of Christ (the Messiah, the Anointed One).**

Thank God we are not left with our own natural weapons, wit, resources, and strength to stand against the enemy. God has armed us with mighty spiritual weapons to overthrow and destroy strongholds. What is interesting is that the word *strongholds* in the original Greek text is the term for "a fortress or castle with thick, impenetrable walls." In the context of this passage, the strongholds being described are fortresses or castles of wrong thinking—not demon spirits, as some have thought.

Strongholds are places in our mind where a particular kind of thought has repeatedly been pondered and accepted, and it now forms a fortress of belief that is strongly defended. Virtually every Christian has a stronghold in some area of their thinking but is unaware of it. As an associate pastor, I've learned from many years of experience that when you attempt to reveal some of these strongholds to help people, they will often fight tooth and nail to hold on to them.

Indeed, it can be an uncomfortable process to admit that we are totally wrong in some of the ways we think. However, if we will identify these patterns of wrong thinking, regardless of how emotionally challenging it can be, those strongholds can be destroyed. Then God's peace will be restored in our lives!

Gain and Maintain Control of Your Thinking

Whether we are actively paying attention or not, our mind will often argue and reason with the truth we know from God's Word. As we saw earlier in Chapter 3, *"...The mind of the flesh [with its carnal thoughts and purposes] is hostile to God, for it does not submit itself to God's Law; indeed it cannot"* (Romans 8:7, AMPC).

Consider this example. Let's say you begin to feel symptoms of sickness in your body. Your natural, fleshly mind will immediately take inventory of your symptoms and remind you of all the sick people you've been around. Then with the aid of the enemy, it will conclude that you have the flu or some other sickness that's going around. Did you know that instead of just accepting the thought, *I'm getting sick*, you can stand against that attack and act on the Word of God?

Let the truth triumph over the enemy's lies! You do this by declaring God's Word out loud over your life and against the enemy. In this case, you can boldly say, "By the stripes Jesus received, I am healed, and no weapon of sickness or disease formed against me will prosper" (see 1 Peter 2:24; Isaiah 54:17).

Of course, your mind—fueled with more falsehoods from the father of lies—will likely continue to argue, offering additional reasons you are getting sick. It will make statements like, *You've really pushed yourself for several weeks, and you haven't eaten well. Besides that, you haven't gotten enough sleep, your body is run down, and your immune system is compromised. You better call in sick and get into bed.*

What I am describing here is what Paul explained in 2 Corinthians 10:5. Your unrenewed mind is offering you arguments, theories, and reasonings in an attempt to talk you out of the healing and protection from sickness that is your inheritance through Christ. These contradicting thoughts are "proud" and "lofty," and they are setting themselves up against the true knowledge of God. What are we to do with such renegade reasonings?

Take Wrong Thoughts Captive!

We are instructed to *"...refute arguments and theories and reasonings and every proud and lofty thing that sets itself up against the [true] knowledge of God; and we lead every thought and purpose away captive into the obedience of Christ (the Messiah, the Anointed One)"* (2 Corinthians 10:5, AMPC).

To effectively stop arguments and reasonings that contradict God's Word, you must learn to become sensitive to the Holy Spirit. He sees and senses with pinpoint accuracy what is coming against you and can teach you the best way to respond. The more time you invest in reading, studying, and meditating on the Word and talking to the Lord in prayer each day, the more sensitive you will become to Him. Then when your mind tries to argue or reason against the Word of God, you can recognize the lie quickly and take it captive into the obedience of Christ!

You can say: "That's not my thought! It's a lie. I resist you, Satan, in the name of Jesus! This is what God says about my situation (speak any Scripture that comes to mind or that you look up that refutes the lie). I choose to believe and stand on the truth of God's Word."

The best time to refute ungodly thoughts is at their onset. Dealing with wrong thoughts as soon as they come will prevent a stronghold from developing. However, if a stronghold has already been built over a period of years, it can still be destroyed through this same method.

Jesus said, *"...If you abide in My word, you are My disciples indeed. And you shall know the truth, and the truth shall make you free"* (John 8:31-32). The way to refute lies, arguments, and reasonings is by knowing and speaking the truth of God's Word. As you diligently meditate on Scripture and pray in the Spirit daily, the truth will set you free from Satan's lies. Every lofty thing that sets itself up against the true knowledge of God will be overthrown.

Four Steps to Walking in God's Peace

There is one more very important passage of Scripture that gives us instructions on controlling our thoughts and staying in peace.

PHILIPPIANS 4:6-9

6 Be anxious for nothing, but in everything by prayer and supplication, with thanksgiving, let your requests be made known to God;

7 And the peace of God, which surpasses all understanding, will guard your hearts and minds through Christ Jesus.

8 Finally, brethren, whatever things are true, whatever things are noble, whatever things are just, whatever things are pure, whatever things are lovely, whatever things are of good report, if there is any virtue and if there is anything praiseworthy—meditate on these things.

9 The things which you learned and received and heard and saw in me, these do, and the God of peace will be with you."

In these verses are four clear steps to walking in the peace of God:

First, refuse to be anxious or worried about anything! Anxiety and worry are forms of fear, and fear is a spirit. We must recognize it, speak to it, and command it to go in the name of Jesus.

Second, pray and make your specific requests known to God. Whatever you are tempted to worry about is what you need to take to the Lord and pray about. Ask Him for wisdom to navigate your way through the situation. He longs to give you answers so that you can live in the victory Jesus provided. Oftentimes, the Holy Spirit will give you a specific Scripture to stand on and speak. Likewise, He may give you instructions on how to handle a situation. Whatever you're walking through, trust that your heavenly Father has the answer, and He wants to give it to you (see James 1:5).

Third, thank and praise God that you have the answer even before you see it. All requests should be accompanied by thanksgiving. This is an act of faith that shows God gratitude for His wisdom and for His peace. Another benefit of thanking the Lord out loud is that your focus gets directed to Him and His goodness rather than on you and your problem. When you thank God, you are magnifying Him, and when you magnify Him, He becomes greater than the problem you're facing. Magnifying God keeps us in a state of trust and pushes all doubt out the door.

Fourth, meditate on or fix your mind on the right things. Always ask yourself, *Are my thoughts lining up with the Word of God? Is what I'm thinking true, noble, just, pure, lovely, of good report, virtuous, or praiseworthy?* If the answer is no, then you must cast those thoughts down! Then meditate on God's thoughts, which are found in His Word. Again and again, your Father tells you He loves you and cares for you. He promised to provide everything you need and make a way out when there seems to be no way.

If you will follow these instructions, you will control your thoughts and begin to experience God's peace!

MY PRAYER CONFESSION OF FAITH:

Lord, forgive me for being double-minded at times and believing the enemy's lies over Your Word. Help me recognize and reject wrong thoughts as soon as they come to my mind and take them captive to the obedience of Christ. I refuse to fret or have anxiety about anything. When I am tempted to worry, I will make specific requests to You in prayer regarding that situation. Then I will thank You and praise You for the great things You've already done and I will meditate on what You promised me in Your Word. I choose to trust You, cast my every care on You, and leave them there. In Your name, Jesus, Amen.

Chapter 5

A Sound Mind

"For God has not given us a spirit of fear, but of power and of love and of a sound mind."

— 2 Timothy 1:7

God's plan for each of us is to have a sound mind. It is His gift to us through the person of the Holy Spirit who lives inside us. A sound mind is a peaceful mind. The devil does not want you or any Christian to live in peace because a sound, peaceful mind is a receiving mind.

When you are anxious, worried, or fearful, it's as if an invisible barrier forms, blocking you from receiving from God. In that troubled state, you can't pay attention to the sermon, regardless of how good it is, and you can't grasp what you're reading in the Bible or hearing from the Holy Spirit. Without a spiritual ear to hear the Word, faith cannot come to you, and without faith, you cannot please God.

In today's world, with all that is going on, a sound mind is exactly what we need to remain peaceful and sane in the midst of insanity.

2 TIMOTHY 1:7 (AMPC)
For God did not give us a spirit of timidity (of cowardice, of craven and cringing and fawning fear), but [He has given us a spirit] of power and of love and of calm and well-balanced mind and discipline and self-control.

First, notice that God has given us a spirit of power. Here, the Greek word for *power* is *dunamis*, which is "explosive, supernatural ability, power, and strength." *Dunamis* is where we get our word dynamite and is the term used to describe "the full force of an advancing army."[1] The fact that this word *dunamis* is used means we have supernatural ability and strength through the Holy Spirit to overcome all anxiety, fear, or depression that comes against us.

In addition to power, God has also given us a spirit of love. In this verse, the word *love* is translated from the Greek word *agape*, which describes "the unconditional, sacrificial God-kind of love." There is no greater love than the *agape* love of God. In fact, it is so powerful, that the Bible says, *"There is no fear in love; but perfect love casts out fear..."* (1 John 4:18). We will discuss this further in Chapter 7.

Along with His love and power, God has given us the gift of a sound mind to effectively fight against fear in all its forms. The Amplified Classic translation reveals that there are four components of a sound mind. These include being calm and well-balanced, along with having discipline and self-control.

A Sound Mind is Calm

A mind that is calm is the opposite of one that is anxious or fearful. Words synonymous with calm include *tranquil*, *peaceful*, *quiet*, and *unruffled*, and one of the primary definitions of calm is "without hurried movement."[2]

Jesus is our great example of a person who lived in a state of calmness. There is not one place in the gospels where He is portrayed as being worried, hurried, or in a rush. Even when news of Lazarus' death reached Him, He did not respond with panic or despair. On the contrary, He waited two more days before going to Bethany to raise Lazarus from the grave.

Personally, I have always been a high-energy, fast-paced person. Even now, my mind sometimes moves faster than my body, making it hard to physically keep up. During my childhood, we did not have all the mental diagnoses that children are labeled with today. If a child was hyperactive, he or she was made to sit down and be still. I think if I were a child today, I would probably be diagnosed with some modern label. Yet despite being energetic and antsy, I always excelled in school because I was able to pay attention long enough to grasp concepts quickly.

Looking back, I now notice that throughout the years, I had to guard against being impatient with people slower than I. Slow drivers were a particular problem for me and often robbed me of peace. I'll never forget one day while driving to church, I found myself getting impatient with a driver in front of me who was moving at a snail's pace. Without realizing it, I had developed the habit of rushing, even though I was never a late person. On that day, the Lord showed me that even if I continued to drive at my current, slower pace, I would still be quite early to church.

When a person feels like they are always being rushed, it is a spirit of fear that is driving them, producing both pressure and anxiety. That is how I used to live years ago, but I made a decision that day to yield to patience and stop allowing myself to be driven to move fast. If you find yourself always rushing around in life, you are not experiencing a sound mind, because soundness of mind is marked by a calm disposition.

Keep in mind that anxiety and worry are forms of fear, and fear is a spirit that can definitely be felt. God does not say we will never feel anxious or fearful. What He promises is a calm (sound) mind as we stay in fellowship with Him.

So even if you feel the presence of fear, it does not have to rattle you or put you into "rush mode." Through faith, you can begin to trust God moment by moment for everything you need, and as a result, you can begin to experience the inheritance of a calm mind and disposition.

ISAIAH 28:16 (KJV)
Therefore thus saith the Lord God, Behold, I lay in Zion for a foundation a stone, a tried stone, a precious corner stone, a sure foundation: he that believeth shall not make haste.

The tried and precious cornerstone mentioned here is Jesus, and the Amplified Classic translation of this verse says, *"...He who believes (trusts in, relies on, and adheres to that Stone) will not be ashamed or give way or hasten away [in sudden panic]."* When you are walking with God and being led by His Spirit, you will not rush or become panicky about situations. As a believer in Christ, you have the promise of becoming like Christ, which means you, too, can remain calm.

A Sound Mind is Well-Balanced

Second Timothy 1:7 also tells us that a sound mind is well-balanced. Without question, balance is vital in numerous areas, including our diet, our budget, and our body itself. What would our life be like without balance? We need it to do just about everything, including standing, walking, and bending down to hug our children.

Likewise, our soul and spirit need balance to be healthy, and the greatest key to experiencing this balance is a steady diet of God's Word. No one can be well-balanced apart from the Word of God. The Bible informs us that God's thoughts are higher than our thoughts.

ISAIAH 55:8-9 (KJV)
8 For my thoughts are not your thoughts, neither are your ways my ways, saith the Lord. 9 For as the heavens are higher than the earth, so are my ways higher than your ways, and my thoughts than your thoughts.

As we take on God's thoughts by reading, studying, and meditating on Scripture, our minds become more well-balanced like His and we begin to think like Him. There is not one person on this planet whose thoughts and ways are better than God's. He is the Supreme Head and Creator of the universe, and a quality life begins when we acknowledge that He is smarter than we are.

Have you ever wondered what made the devil become the devil? The Bible tells us that there was a time when Lucifer (the devil) became convinced in his heart that his thoughts were higher and greater than God's. The Bible calls this "iniquity"—a word that means *unrighteousness, injustice,* or *perversity*—and it was this arrogant thinking that was Lucifer's undoing.

ISAIAH 14:12-15 (KJV)
12 How art thou fallen from heaven, O Lucifer, son of the morning! how art thou cut down to the ground, which didst weaken the nations!
13 For thou hast said in thine heart, I will ascend into heaven, I will exalt my throne above the stars of God: I will sit also upon the mount of the congregation, in the sides of the north:
14 I will ascend above the heights of the clouds; I will be like the most High.
15 Yet thou shalt be brought down to hell, to the sides of the pit.

Lucifer's thoughts were not God's thoughts. They were his own selfish and destructive ideas. Did you know that every time we choose our thoughts over God's thoughts, we are doing the same thing Lucifer did? We are, in a sense, exalting our reasoning above God's thinking. If we make any thought a higher priority than God's thoughts, we are saying we know better than God does, and things will not end well for us either.

I believe this is one of the reasons Peter urges us, *"Be well balanced (temperate, sober of mind), be vigilant and cautious at all times; for that enemy of yours, the devil, roams around like a lion roaring [in fierce hunger], seeking someone to seize upon and devour"* (1 Peter 5:8, AMPC).

If you ever come to a place where it seems you know better and you have it all together, think again. There is only one God, and He always prevails. It is futile to fight against the truth—so embrace it! The more you allow the truth of God's Word to permeate your mind and heart, the more well-balanced your thinking will be, and the more you will enjoy God's peace.

A Sound Mind is Disciplined

True freedom only comes from discipline. Without discipline, bondage to wrong thinking, wrong speaking, and wrong behavior is inevitable. I know that discipline seems to have become a dirty word in our society today. Many people have cast off restraint, living undisciplined lives, and they want to be applauded for it. However, if they would study the lives of those who lack discipline and compare them to people who exercise great discipline, they would see the value of developing this life-giving virtue.

Discipline can be defined as "the practice of training to obey a code of behavior."[3] It is developed by instructing, educating, and informing the mind in correct principles and habits.[4] If we will practice taking control of our thoughts, we will develop a behavior pattern that stops fear and anxiety before it takes hold in our minds.

I had to practice responding in the right way to wrong thoughts and situations to keep anxiety from taking control of my life. From the time I was very young until the time I was attacked with panic, I always responded to negative situations with racing thoughts. Few people knew what I was thinking because I usually didn't display my feelings. However, after I was delivered from anxiety at age 30, it became clear that I needed to continually police—or discipline—my mind in order to stay in peace.

ISAIAH 26:3 (NLT)
You will keep in perfect peace all who trust in you, all whose thoughts are fixed on you!

By spending adequate time meditating on Scriptures, I learned how to take wrong thoughts captive as they came and replace them with what God's Word says.

In the first few years after being set free from panic attacks, feelings of anxiety would frequently try to come back. But by disciplining my mind, I grew stronger and stronger at refuting mental attacks and maintaining my peace. Now, decades later, I rarely even feel anxious about anything. How is that possible? Through faith in God's Word and through the practice of training the mind how to respond to thoughts and situations that arise. Simply stated, I have learned to trust my heavenly Father in a way I did not trust Him in the past!

I cannot promise you an instantaneous deliverance from anxiety and depression. What I can guarantee is that if you will learn God's Word, hold tightly to it, and don't give up, anxiety and depression will eventually be pushed out of your life! The key is abiding in fellowship with Jesus daily and being willing to yield to the promptings of His Spirit living in you.

> **HEBREWS 12:10-11 (NLT)**
> **10 God's discipline is always good for us, so that we might share in his holiness.**
> **11 No discipline is enjoyable while it is happening—it's painful! But afterward there will be a peaceful harvest of right living for those who are trained in this way.**

Developing discipline leads to experiencing success in every area of your life. Through your cooperation with the Holy Spirit, supernatural discipline will be established in your life, enabling you to live free of anxiety, worry, fear, and depression.

A Sound Mind Is Self-Controlled

According to Webster's dictionary, *self-control* is defined as "restraint exercised over one's own impulses, emotions, or desires."[5] Words equivalent to self-control include *willpower*, *restraint*, and *self-discipline*.

Self-control is actually one of the nine fruits of the Spirit. If you are a child of God, you have the ability to exercise self-control, whether you have felt like it or not. That means through the power of the Holy Spirit living in you, you can stop giving in to feelings of fear, worry, anxiety, and depression.

GALATIANS 5:22-25
22 But the fruit of the Spirit is love, joy, peace, longsuffering, kindness, goodness, faithfulness,
23 Gentleness, self-control. Against such there is no law.
24 And those who are Christ's have crucified the flesh with its passions and desires.
25 If we live in the Spirit, let us also walk in the Spirit.

I want to draw your attention to verse 24, which says that if we are Christ's, we have crucified our flesh with its passions and desires. To crucify means "to put to death, utterly destroy, or extinguish." That is what God's Word instructs us to do with the passions and desires of our old nature.

Now, when most people think of passions and desires, they imagine lustful or wicked things. But there is more to these words than you might think. The Greek word for *passions* is *pathema*, and it describes "an affliction or pain of the mind or emotions." It is often translated *affliction* or *suffering* in the New Testament. Equally important is the Greek word for *desires*, which is *epithumia*, and it means "a longing or craving for what is forbidden."

Crucifying the flesh does not just include extinguishing forbidden longings. It also includes not letting the influence of thoughts or emotions take charge of us. Anxiety and depression are spiritual influences that seek to gain access to and take control over our mind and emotions. According to Galatians 5:22-25, the Holy Spirit has given us the fruit of self-control, and it empowers us to crucify fleshly impulses and influences.

Hardship and pain can certainly influence our thoughts and emotions. Many cases of anxiety and depression stem from events in life that were difficult and painful. At the same time, there are also plenty of instances of anxiety and depression that did not come from hardship or pain. They simply came because of believing wrong thoughts. In either case, a believer has the power to overcome these influences.

How do we do it? Galatians 5:25 gives us the answer: *"If we live in the Spirit, let us also walk in the Spirit."* The way to walk in the Spirit is to yield to the Spirit's promptings. The Spirit of God will never lead you into anxiety or depression. He will always remind you of what God's Word says. He will prompt you to use the spiritual authority Jesus has given you[6] to take captive every thought and imagination that doesn't line up with the truth.

At the first sign of anxiety or fear...

1. Speak to it. Say, "Anxiety! Fear! I resist you in the name of Jesus. I refuse to fear or be anxious. God has not given me a spirit of fear, but of power, love, and a sound mind. I command you to leave now!"

2. Worship Jesus. He is your wonderful Deliverer and Healer. As you worship, it will only be a very short time, and the influence or emotion of anxiety and fear will leave.

The same process works for feelings of sadness or depression. When you sense these coming against you, speak to it and say, "Sadness! Depression! I resist you in the name of Jesus! I refuse to be hurt, offended, sad, or depressed. God has given me the oil of joy for mourning and the garment of praise for the spirit of heaviness (see Isaiah 61:3). You must leave now!"

Remember, the Bible says, *"...We have the mind of Christ (the Messiah) and do hold the thoughts (feelings and purposes) of His heart"* (1 Corinthians 2:16, AMPC). If we are born again, His Spirit lives inside our spirit, and therefore, our spirit-man thinks like Him. To develop the mind of Christ in our soul—which is our mind, will, and emotions—we must continue to abide in God's Word and make His thoughts our thoughts.

The more we practice standing against anxiety, fear, and depression at their onset and the more we worship Jesus, the more skillful we will become! Likewise, the more we embrace God's thoughts and His ways, which are found in His Word, the more soundness of mind we will possess, and the more success we will have.

MY PRAYER CONFESSION OF FAITH:

Lord, Your Word says that You have given me a spirit of power, love, and a sound mind, and that I have the mind of Christ. I choose to believe that and only yield to sound thinking and to speak sound words that keep me in peace. Help me feed on Your Word, making Your thoughts become my thoughts. I choose to live calm, well-balanced, disciplined, and self-controlled. In Your name, Jesus, Amen.

[1] Renner, Rick. Sparkling Gems from the Greek 2 (Tulsa, OK; Institute Books, 2016) p. 1087.

[2] Definition of calm (https://dictionary.cambridge.org/us/dictionary/english/calm; accessed 6/28/24).

[3] Definition of discipline (https://www.oxfordreference.com/display/10.1093/oi/authority.20110803095721587; accessed 7/15/24).

[4] Adapted from American Dictionary of the English Language, Noah Webster 1828 (San Francisco, CA: Foundation for American Christian Education, 1967, 1995).

[5] Definition of self-control (https://www.merriam-webster.com/dictionary/self-control; accessed 7/1/24).

[6] See Luke 10:19.

SECTION 3

THREE THINGS THAT EXPEL FEAR AND PRODUCE PEACE

Chapter 6

The Power of Praise

"Through Him, therefore, let us constantly and at all times offer up to God a sacrifice of praise, which is the fruit of lips that thankfully acknowledge and confess and glorify His name."

– Hebrews 13:15 (AMPC)

Perhaps one of the most helpful actions for overcoming anxiety and particularly depression is praising God. When we make the decision to praise Him, His Holy Spirit comes upon us in a powerful way. The Bible says, He gives us *"...beauty for ashes, the oil of joy for mourning, the garment of praise for the spirit of heaviness; that [we] may be called trees of righteousness, the planting of the Lord, that He may be glorified"* (Isaiah 61:3).

If you are dealing with a "spirit of heaviness," praise is one of the greatest scriptural solutions to overcome it. You may not feel like it, and your circumstances may be screaming that it is a useless, foolish activity in which to engage. Nevertheless, if you will push past your feelings and what you see in the natural and will praise God long enough, you will be delivered from anything the devil brings against you.

Begin with Giving Thanks

In Psalm 16:11, David declared to the Lord, *"...In Your presence is fullness of joy; at Your right hand are pleasures forevermore."* When we get into God's presence, amazing things happen. We receive an infilling of His joy and His goodness that permeates every area of our life.

Getting into His presence starts with being thankful. God's Word says, *"Enter into His gates with thanksgiving..."* (Psalm 100:4). When things are not going well and we've been hit by one disappointment after another, it is hard to be thankful. Bad news, bills, and challenges do not create warm, fuzzy feelings of gratitude. It is in those moments that we must purposely choose to look for things for which to be thankful.

The good news is God's blessings are all around you! For example, is your heart beating and are your lungs breathing? You can thank God. Do you have clothes to wear, shoes on your feet, and a home in which to live? You have more reasons to offer thanks. Do you have food to eat and clean water to drink? Again, thank God. Do you have people in your life that love you and a church family that cares about you? Then you have even more reasons to thank the Lord.

Oftentimes, I tell God how thankful I am to be saved, healed, and delivered from the power of Satan. Likewise, I tell Jesus that He's a wonderful Healer and Deliverer, and I thank Him for His shed blood and the price He paid for my freedom. You will find that once you begin giving thanks, the list of things to thank God for keeps growing. And as you thank Him, the tension and sadness will lift and be replaced with appreciation for His goodness. Hope will be restored, along with an anticipation that He will come through for you once again in your current situation.

Thankfulness Will Give Way to Praise

While thanking God gets us into His gates, praise ushers us even closer into His courts.

> **PSALM 100:4 (AMPC)**
> **Enter into His gates with thanksgiving and a thank offering and into His courts with praise! Be thankful and say so to Him, bless and affectionately praise His name!**

This passage makes it clear that thanking God and praising Him go hand in hand. They work together to bring God glory and bring us closer and closer to His manifest presence. Although the Spirit of God is always with us because we are born-again believers, God's manifest presence is profoundly different. Praise creates an environment for God's manifest presence to come.

One Bible verse that explains the power of praise is Psalm 22:3, which tells us that God *"inhabits the praises"* of His people. The word *inhabits* in the original Hebrew text means "to sit enthroned." So, when the Bible says God inhabits the praises of His people, it is a picture of His presence *sitting* or *resting on top of a person or congregation* who is praising Him. As we sincerely worship God from our hearts, we create an atmosphere that magnetically attracts Him to us, and when He comes, He begins to manifest His glory.

All throughout the Old Testament, there are examples of God's glory manifesting. One of the most memorable moments was when Solomon and the people of Israel dedicated the newly built temple. As the people worshiped and offered sacrifices to God, His glory descended and filled the temple. His presence was so powerful the priests couldn't continue their tasks.

That's what happens when you and I push all our negative feelings aside and choose to praise God from our heart. Our sacrifice of praise welcomes Him, and His glory arrives on the scene, bringing with it all His goodness and His delivering power.

Paul and Silas experienced this power in a Macedonian prison. Rather than sink in despair after being beaten and placed in chains, they chose to pray and sing praises to God. Their praise invited God's presence, and the Bible says, *"Suddenly there was a great earthquake, so that the foundations of the prison were shaken; and immediately all the doors were opened and everyone's chains were loosed"* (Acts 16:26). When their praises went up, God's tangible glory came down, delivering Paul and Silas from bondage and bringing salvation to the jailer and his entire household.

That's what praising God does. Your praise creates a seat on which God sits and rests, bringing His life-transforming power, peace, and freedom into your life.

Praising God Maximizes His Power
and Minimizes Our Problems

Many people have confidently announced their ability for multi-tasking in life. However, there is no such thing as true multi-tasking, because the human brain cannot think two thoughts at the same time. When people declare that they can multi-task, what they are really saying is that they can bounce back and forth quickly between two activities.

Although there would certainly be some benefits to being able to do two things at once, when it comes to overcoming anxiety and depression, it's a good thing we can't. The fact is, it is impossible to think about how hopeless our situation is and praise God simultaneously. Only one thing can be done at a time.

Praising God puts our focus on Him and His greatness rather than on us and the problems we're facing. I believe David was well aware of this truth, which is why he declared, *"I will bless the Lord at all times; His praise shall continually be in my mouth"* (Psalm 34:1).

Now, I realize that when we are feeling depressed or anxious, the last thing we "feel" like doing is praising God. This is where exercising self-control and yielding to the Holy Spirit—who is living in us—comes in. With His strength, we can choose to stand against the heaviness of depression and the fear that wants to keep us down, and like Paul and Silas, we can lift our hands and our voice and give praise to God.

I have done this time and time again in my own life. Although I was delivered from anxiety many years ago, the enemy has still come against me many times—especially at night—trying to regain access into my life. In those moments, when I was overtaken with a sudden sense of anxiety, it was as though I could feel the enemy tiptoeing in the distance just waiting for me to cower and collapse under the weight of his attack.

But even though I felt anxious, I refused to give in to it. Instead, I said, "I refuse to fear in Jesus' name. I resist you, spirit of fear. You have no authority in my life, and you must leave me now!" Then I raised my hands and began to praise the Lord, repeatedly saying things like, "I love You, Jesus! And I worship You, Jesus! You are my strength, my peace, and my Deliverer, and I put my trust in You!"

As I continued to praise God, within minutes, the feelings of anxiety disappeared—every time without fail. I have heard testimonies of people that were healed of incurable diseases by simply spending their free time praising and worshiping the Lord. Indeed, praise is the highest form of prayer we can offer, because praise requires faith, and it is through faith we obtain God's promises.

God Hears Our Prayers and Responds to Our Praise

As you step out in faith and begin to praise God, a supernatural strength will arise within you. His anointing will always show up when you act in faith. As His strength increases in you, His Spirit will enable you to continue to praise and worship God with ease for an extended period of time. Again, if you will praise God long enough, you will be delivered from anything the devil brings against you—including anxiety, worry, fear, and depression.

> **PSALM 40:1-4**
> 1 I waited patiently for the Lord; and He inclined to me, and heard my cry.
> 2 He also brought me up out of a horrible pit, out of the miry clay, and set my feet upon a rock, and established my steps.
> 3 He has put a new song in my mouth—praise to our God; many will see it and fear, and will trust in the Lord.
> 4 Blessed is that man who makes the Lord his trust...

People who complain will remain in their pitiful condition. Those who cry out to God in prayer and with praise will be raised out of it. As children of God, we must keep an attitude of gratitude, always looking for things for which we can thank Him and praise Him. That's the principle of Psalm 77:11-12 (NIV), where the psalmist said, *"I will remember the deeds of the Lord; yes, I will remember your miracles of long ago. I will consider all your works and meditate on all your mighty deeds."*

If you are having difficulty finding something to praise God for, pray and ask Him to help you begin remembering all the many ways He has blessed your life. Ask Him to show you some of the many times He protected you, provided for you, forgave you, and had mercy on you. The fact is He has abundantly blessed you with everything you need to live this life and carry out your calling.

EPHESIANS 1:3 (NIV)
Praise be to the God and Father of our Lord Jesus Christ, who has blessed us in the heavenly realms with every spiritual blessing in Christ.

2 PETER 1:3 (NLT)
By his divine power, God has given us everything we need for living a godly life. We have received all of this by coming to know him, the one who called us to himself by means of his marvelous glory and excellence.

I encourage you to make a decision to never again let anxiety, fear, or depression dominate your life. Instead, choose to stand against it. When you feel those familiar feelings trying to come on you, open your mouth and begin to thank and praise God for all the good things He's done. Resist the spirit of fear and depression in the name of Jesus, and it will flee!

MY PRAYER CONFESSION OF FAITH:

Lord, when anxiety and fear try to take hold of my mind, I will resist them, trust You, and look for things for which to be thankful. When sadness and depression are coming against me, I will push past how I feel and what I see and praise You anyway. You are a faithful and mighty Deliverer! And I choose to trust You, to thank You, and to praise You for all the kindness and goodness You've shown me. I resist the spirit of fear and welcome Your manifest presence in my life. In Your name, Jesus, Amen.

Chapter 7

The Father's Love

"There is no fear in love; but perfect love casts out fear...."

— 1 John 4:18

As we have noted, anxiety and worry—as well as depression—are all expressions of fear. Thankfully, there is a remedy for these debilitating emotions, and that remedy is the love of God. I am convinced that until we receive a revelation of the love of our heavenly Father toward us, we will never really enjoy our privileges as His sons and daughters. And one of the greatest privileges is living free from fear in all its forms.

Before Adam and Eve's fall in Eden, fear did not exist. They only knew the loving, peaceful presence of the Father. God's original plan for mankind was to live in perfect peace. Adam and Eve enjoyed that peace for a season, but after they disobeyed God by believing the serpent's word instead of God's word, everything changed.

In that moment, sin and death entered the world, and their intimate fellowship with the Lord was broken. For the first time, the torment of fear was felt. With their eyes now opened to evil, Adam and Eve saw themselves in a way God never intended. When they heard Him walking in the garden, they hid themselves from His presence.

> **GENESIS 3:9-10**
> **9   Then the Lord God called to Adam and said to him, 'Where are you?'**
> **10 So he said, 'I heard Your voice in the garden, and I was afraid because I was naked; and I hid myself.'**

Adam's first words to God after he sinned were, *"I was afraid."* The fact that he was afraid and went into hiding tells us that sin had damaged his view of the Father. The "perfect love" that casts out all fear was forgotten, and an unhealthy fear took love's place, bringing with it the tormenting thought of punishment (see 1 John 4:18).

The Enemy Starts Early

If you have dealt with fear, you know it can be tormenting. Satan is the master manipulator who uses fear to bring about his plans in people's lives. In a subtle but cruel way, he begins injecting fear into individuals at a very young age through their various childhood experiences, so that they develop the habit of responding to things in fear.

Paul identified Satan as *"the prince of the power of the air"* in Ephesians 2:2, and in our day, we can clearly see why. Using the airwaves, he sneaks up on children through music, television programming, blockbuster movies, and social media, all of which contribute to the development of fear in their lives.

When I was a child, a very popular series of monster movies was broadcast on a television program called "Creature Features." These classic, black and white films, which were originally produced in the 1930s and 1940s, included *Frankenstein*, *Dracula*, and many others. By today's standards, these movies seem primitive and tame. At that time, however, they were very scary for most children to watch.

For the record, my mother did not allow us to watch these films, and rightfully so. Unfortunately, I had disobeyed her by occasionally watching them during sleepovers at a friend's house, where they were allowed. As a result, I suffered all kinds of nightmares for several years after watching those movies. Again and again, I would dream that monsters were in my closet, under my bed, and roaming the house just waiting to come out at night and kill us.

Making an even more disturbing impact was the 1973 movie *The Exorcist*. Since it carried an R rating, I was not old enough to see it when it debuted. But a few years later, I somehow got into a theater and watched it. To this day, there are images from the film that are deeply troubling to see. I was so filled with fear because of that movie that if the theme song came on the radio when I was alone in the house, I would run outside. Thankfully, as a Catholic girl, I had enough sense to know the devil is real, and I wanted nothing to do with him.

Today, computer generated effects in horror movies are extremely advanced, making violence, bloodshed, and things connected with darkness seem incredibly realistic. And these "fear flicks" are also very popular. The fact is many people love to be scared. There is a certain "high" that can be experienced while watching frightening things. When fear registers in the brain, all sorts of hormones and neurotransmitters are released, creating a chemical high that can become quite addictive. I have personally known people who had an addiction to horror movies. The enticement of fear in such media—not to mention haunted houses and other paranormal experiences—is Satan's bait to take people captive and hold them in bondage to fear.

While the effects of horror movies may seem silly or insignificant to talk about, my point is that fear is introduced to us at a very early age, and in my case, it set me up for greater fears in my future. Remember, fear is a spirit sent out from Satan to gain access to and control over our life. As a parent, I would never allow my children to be exposed to this demonic influence, and I would encourage you to do likewise.

Where Are You Putting Your Faith? In What the *Devil* Says or What *God* Says?

During my childhood, I had no revelation about the love of God or the authority of the believer. And like countless others, that lack of knowledge was destroying the peace and soundness of mind that God wants us all to have. The truth is,

I seemed to have more faith in the power of the devil than in the power of God, which is how many Christians live today.

It has been said that *fear* is **F**alse **E**vidence **A**ppearing **R**eal, and if you think about it, there is much truth to this statement. Fear of the *possible* outcome of situations is what causes most anxiety and depression. People hear news reports, doctor's reports, etc., and often get anxious and begin to worry that something bad is going to happen. Something bad may have already happened, but our natural inclination is to believe that things will get even worse. Satan capitalizes on the situation by bringing us fearful thoughts and imaginations, which attempt to convince us that there is no way out of the bad situation we are in.

If we swallow all the negative "what-if" scenarios that enter our mind, a sense of hopelessness will set in, and like dark storm clouds, it will hover over us for as long as we let it. Like a hamster running aimlessly in a rat wheel, we will become exhausted by discouragement, and then depression will set in, all because we refuse to believe that things can change and good things can happen.

It is understandable that an unbeliever would have problems with fear, but believers in Jesus should never have to live another tormented day in their lives. Fear is only possible when we believe what the devil is threatening more than we believe that God truly loves us and that He has good for us. He Himself declares, *"...I know the thoughts that I think toward you, says the Lord, thoughts of peace and not of evil, to give you a future and a hope"* (Jeremiah 29:11).

No child of God should ever live with feelings of discouragement and hopelessness about anything. Yes, in this life we will experience troubles. That is what Jesus said in John 16:33. But we can't leave out what He said immediately after that in the very same verse, *"...But be of good cheer, I have overcome the world."*

Friend, you have the Greater One living inside of you! First John 4:4 says, *"You are of God, little children, and have overcome them, because He who is in you is greater than he who is in the world."* Your heavenly Father not only has the answer for every situation, but He also longs to share those answers with you and show you the way out. That is what love will do for you.

God Loves You!
Yes, *You!*

Do you remember the song "Jesus Loves Me"? It was originally a poem written in 1860 by Anna Bartlett Warner to comfort a dying child and later became one of the most popular Christian songs in churches around the world.[1] In 1862, William Bradbury tweaked the words, added the refrain, and placed the song in his popular hymnal.[2] You may remember the first stanza and the chorus:

"Jesus loves me, this I know,
For the Bible tells me so;
Little ones to Him belong,
They are weak, but He is strong.

Refrain:
> Yes, Jesus loves me,
> Yes, Jesus loves me,
> Yes, Jesus loves me,
> The Bible tells me so!"[3]

So simple—yet so profound. Jesus loves you—yes, *YOU!* May those words sink deep into your soul and spirit and forever change the way you see Him and His view of you.

It seems that very few of us have difficulty believing that the Father loves other people or that He loves His only begotten Son, Jesus. What we struggle to believe is that He truly loves us—but He does! In fact, in Jesus' final prayer before enduring the cross, He Himself said that God the Father loves you and me **just as much** as He loves Him [Jesus] (see John 17:23).

"How is that possible?" you ask. It is all because of Jesus. He is *in* the Father, and the Father is *in* Him. And we are united together *in them* (see John 17:21-23). We are all one with Christ and *in* Christ, so when the Father looks at you, He sees Jesus! That's how **He loves you just as much as He loves Jesus**—because you are one with Christ (see Galatians 3:28; 1 Corinthians 12:13).

Paul Prayed That We Would Personally Know and Experience God's Love

The apostle Paul knew the crucial importance of understanding the love of God. In fact, it is so imperative that one of the prayers he wrote and prayed for believers is all about being rooted in God's love.

EPHESIANS 3:16-19 (AMPC)

16 May He grant you out of the rich treasury of His glory to be strengthened and reinforced with mighty power in the inner man by the [Holy] Spirit [Himself indwelling your innermost being and personality].

17 May Christ through your faith [actually] dwell (settle down, abide, make His permanent home) in your hearts! May you be rooted deep in love and founded securely on love,

18 That you may have the power and be strong to apprehend and grasp with all the saints [God's devoted people, the experience of that love] what is the breadth and length and height and depth [of it];

19 [That you may really come] to know [practically, through experience for yourselves] the love of Christ, which far surpasses mere knowledge [without experience]; that you may be filled [through all your being] unto all the fullness of God [may have the richest measure of the divine Presence, and become a body wholly filled and flooded with God Himself]!

To gain and retain more fully the benefits of this very powerful prayer, let's take some time to break it down into its unique parts and meditate on each truth being presented.

Five Specific Requests
Paul Prayed on Our Behalf

First, Paul prayed that *"…Christ through your faith [actually] dwell (settle down, abide, make His permanent home) in your hearts!"* For all who put their faith in Jesus and His completed work on the cross, and who live by His Word, He promised to come and live inside them (see John 14:23). And where Christ is, fear cannot stay. Indeed, He has promised to never leave us or forsake us (see Hebrews 13:5). We are the permanent home of His Holy Spirit (see 1 Corinthians 3:16), and it is His Spirit, indwelling your innermost being and personality, that strengthens and reinforces you with mighty power in your inner man.

Second, Paul prayed that *"…You be rooted deep in love and founded securely on love."* The "love" being referred to here is the Greek word *agape*, which is the unconditional, God-kind of love that never fails. The more we are rooted in Jesus' love, the more we will know in our hearts and personally experience His patience, kindness, and goodness. His love keeps no record of our wrongs, believes the best, and hopes in all things. The more deeply rooted in God's *agape* love we become, the less fear we will have. His peace will push fear away and begin to dominate our every day.

Third, Paul asked God, *"That you may have the power and be strong to apprehend and grasp with all the saints [God's devoted people, the experience of that love] what is the breadth and length and height and depth [of it]"*. The word *apprehend* means "to grab hold of, possess, and make one's own." It takes mental, emotional, and spiritual strength to *apprehend* the experience of God's love.

The reason it takes strong faith to receive His love is because His love is beyond human comprehension. I think we all know we don't deserve God's love, and consequently, many people subconsciously reject His love. The truth is that God doesn't love us because we deserve it. His love cannot be earned. He freely gives us His love, which is what *agape* love does. It gives what cannot be earned.

The Bible says, *"God shows and clearly proves His [own] love for us by the fact that while we were still sinners, Christ (the Messiah, the Anointed One) died for us"* (Romans 5:8). The greater the revelation of God's love that we have, the more we allow Him to love us like He wants to, and the more we will experience the results of His love. Those results include His forgiveness, peace, and joy, as well as His healing and restoration of body, mind, and emotions.

The fourth request Paul prayed was, *"[That you may really come] to know [practically, through experience for yourselves] the love of Christ, which far surpasses mere knowledge [without experience]...."* Although we can gain knowledge about the love of Christ from reading the Bible, *experiencing* His love far surpasses just having head knowledge about it. As we personally experience the love of Christ, we are filled with the fullness of who He is—which is an intangible gift that cannot be taken away.

The fifth and final thing Paul prayed was, *"...That you may be filled [through all your being] unto all the fullness of God [may have the richest measure of the divine Presence, and become a body wholly filled and flooded with God Himself]!"* The greater the measure of the presence of God in our life, the more we will experience all that He is. When we are completely filled with His divine presence, there is no room left for anxiety, fear, sorrow, or depression. Instead, we are filled with love, joy, peace, kindness, and goodness—not to mention health, power, and prosperity.

I encourage you to pray Ephesians 3:16-19 daily—for yourself, your family, and for other believers. It is a scriptural prayer and one that God will most definitely answer. The more you pray these verses, the more you will understand God's love and begin to see His Word come to pass in your life.

To Live Free from Fear
You Need a Deeper Revelation of God's Love

Fear—in all its various forms—is a lack of faith in God's Word and a lack of revelation of His love. If we are dealing with fear, we lack the intimate knowledge of God's character. Simply put, we don't fully know who He is.

Most Christians believe that God can heal and deliver, but they do not believe He will assuredly do it for them. Sadly, they often swallow the lie that they have not been good enough or that they don't have enough faith to receive His help. This mistaken belief comes as a result of not spending enough quality time with the Father.

For instance, a person who is afraid they won't be healed or afraid they won't have enough money to pay their bills is really believing their heavenly Father won't come through for them. Similarly, a person who fears being left alone if their spouse should die is not trusting that their heavenly Father will never leave them nor forsake them. When someone is in fear like this, they subconsciously believe God is withholding something from them or that they are being punished because they did something wrong. Fear brings with it the thought of punishment or torment.

The answer in all such situations is to receive a deeper revelation of God's love.

The apostle John, who often refers to himself as "the one whom Jesus loved," had much to say about the love of God. One of the most important principles he wrote is found here:

1 JOHN 4:18 (AMPC)
There is no fear in love [dread does not exist], but full-grown (complete, perfect) love turns fear out of doors and expels every trace of terror! For fear brings with it the thought of punishment, and [so] he who is afraid has not reached the full maturity of love [is not yet grown into love's complete perfection].

In this passage, the Holy Spirit is speaking through John and telling us that if we are afraid, we have not reached full maturity in God's love. Just as our faith can grow and develop, so can the *agape* love of God in us. The Bible says,

"…God is love" (1 John 4:8). Yes, God has love and He gives love. But most importantly, God *is* love. It is not just something He does—it is the essence of who He is.

We Can Mature in God's Love

The more we get to know God—Who is love—the more we will mature in His love. This is a process that takes place over time as we live in fellowship with Him.

> **1 JOHN 4:12 (AMPC)**
> No man has at any time [yet] seen God. But if we love one another, God abides (lives and remains) in us and His love (that love which is essentially His) is brought to completion (to its full maturity, runs its full course, is perfected) in us!

Here we see that one of the ways God's love matures and is brought to completion in us is by us loving one another.

> **1 JOHN 4:16-17 (AMPC)**
> 16 …God is love, and he who dwells and continues in love dwells and continues in God, and God dwells and continues in him.
> 17 In this [union and communion with Him] love is brought to completion and attains perfection with us….

The other way God's love matures and is brought to completion in us is by spending time in fellowship with Him. Again, it is God's perfected, full-grown love in us that pushes fear out the door and expels every trace of terror!

Do you want to experience freedom from fear? Spend time with *Love* (God) every chance you get. Sit in His presence. Reflect on His goodness. Thank Him for His faithfulness. Praise Him for His wonderful works. Invest time in His Word—reading, studying, and meditating on it. And serve Him with gladness! These are the basic steps to building a relationship with Him.

As you grow in your knowledge of the Father's love, you will personally see how He always provides, protects, and takes care of you—even in times of trouble. Fear will lose its grip on you and no longer have a place in your mind and emotions. Peace will begin to rule in its place.

The Biggest Fear of All Is No Match for Jesus!

Hopefully you are beginning to see that people who have a revelation of God's love are fearless. They have no fear of negative circumstances because they believe God's love will always deliver them. Therefore, anxiety, worry, dread, and panic do not exist in their life.

Even the fear of death, which is the granddaddy of all fears, is no match for Jesus. Let's face it: The fear of dying is the ultimate fear that often lurks in the background of our lives. It is common to every human, regardless of one's level of education, wealth, or standing in society.

Jesus was aware of this overarching fear that plagues humanity, which is one of the reasons He became human and experienced all that He did.

HEBREWS 2:14-15 (AMPC)

**14 Since, therefore, [these His] children share in
flesh and blood [in the physical nature of human
beings], He [Himself] in a similar manner partook
of the same [nature], that by [going through]
death He might bring to nought and make of no
effect him who had the power of death—that is,
the devil—**

**15 And also that He might deliver and completely
set free all those who through the [haunting] fear
of death were held in bondage throughout the
whole course of their lives.**

Please don't miss what God's Word is saying here.
This passage is telling us that Jesus became human and
experienced death, and in doing so, He defeated the devil
who had the power of death. But that's not all. Jesus also
delivered us from *the fear of death*! Through our faith in
Him, we are completely set free and no longer held hostage
to the fear of dying!

For a believer in Christ, death no longer has a sting
(see 1 Corinthians 15:54-55). To be absent from the body is to
be present with the Lord (see 2 Corinthians 5:8). How can we
experience this deliverance from the fear of death that Jesus
paid for with His life? Again, it all comes down to receiving a
heart revelation of God's love.

Nothing Can Separate You from God's Love!

The more you get to know God—Who is love—the more
you will mature in His love. Even the renowned apostle Paul,

who wrote nearly two-thirds of the New Testament, had to grow in his understanding of God's love. He asked,

ROMANS 8:35 (NLT)
Can anything ever separate us from Christ's love? Does it mean he no longer loves us if we have trouble or calamity, or are persecuted, or hungry, or destitute, or in danger, or threatened with death?

Through Paul's ongoing fellowship with the Father, he discovered a life-changing truth all of us need to know.

ROMANS 8:37-39 (NLT)
37 ...Despite all these things, overwhelming victory is ours through Christ, who loved us.
38 And I am convinced that nothing can ever separate us from God's love. Neither death nor life, neither angels nor demons, neither our fears for today nor our worries about tomorrow—not even the powers of hell can separate us from God's love.
39 No power in the sky above or in the earth below—indeed, nothing in all creation will ever be able to separate us from the love of God that is revealed in Christ Jesus our Lord.

A growing revelation of the Father's love is exactly what you need to break free from all fear. To help you mature in His love and experience this freedom, begin to pray this prayer daily, which is taken directly from Ephesians 3:16-19.

MY PRAYER CONFESSION OF FAITH:

Father, strengthen and reinforce me with mighty power in my inner man by Your Holy Spirit who dwells in my innermost being and personality.

May Christ, through my faith, settle down, abide, and make His permanent home in my heart! And may I be rooted deep in and founded securely on Your love.

Please give me the power and strength to apprehend and fully grasp with all Christians the experience of Your love, enabling me to personally understand the breadth, length, height, and depth of it.

Enable me to really come to know practically, through personal experience, the love of Christ, which far surpasses mere knowledge without experience. And fill me through all my being with all the fullness of You—may I have the richest measure of Your divine Presence and become a body wholly filled and flooded with You!

In Jesus' name, Amen!

[1] Jesus Loves Me (https://en.wikipedia.org/wiki/Jesus_Loves_Me; accessed 7/18/24). 2. Ibid. 3. Ibid.

Chapter 8

The Secret Place

"He who dwells in the secret place of the Most High shall remain stable and fixed under the shadow of the Almighty [Whose power no foe can withstand].

— Psalm 91:1 (AMPC)

As believers, the way we are equipped and prepared to walk in the peace that Jesus paid for is by abiding in the *secret place*. David refers to this amazing place of power, protection, and peace in various places throughout the Psalms.

- In Psalm 32:7, it is our *hiding place*.

- In Psalm 27:5, it is the *secret of His tabernacle* (or *tent*).

- In Psalm 31:20, it is the *secret place of His presence*.

Psalm 91:1 (AMPC) declares, *"He who dwells in the secret place of the Most High shall remain stable and fixed under the shadow of the Almighty [Whose power no foe can withstand]."*

Our secret place is *Jesus*. The moment we invite Him to be our Lord and Savior, His Holy Spirit takes up residency in our heart and we are placed *in Christ*—safe and secure, out of the enemy's reach (see 1 Corinthians 1:30). Learning to abide in Him is a major key to experiencing freedom from anxiety, fear, and depression and to receiving all the blessings He has provided.

Jesus Wants Vibrant Fellowship with You

There is an amazing parallel between "dwelling in the secret place," which is talked about in Psalm 91, and "abiding in Christ," which Jesus Himself teaches us to do in John 15. Just hours before enduring the Roman scourge and being crucified on the cross, Jesus gave His followers—which includes us—these vital instructions:

> **JOHN 15:4-7 (AMPC)**
> **4 Dwell in Me, and I will dwell in you. [Live in Me, and I will live in you.] Just as no branch can bear fruit of itself without abiding in (being vitally united to) the vine, neither can you bear fruit unless you abide in Me.**
> **5 I am the Vine; you are the branches. Whoever lives in Me and I in him bears much (abundant) fruit. However, apart from Me [cut off from vital union with Me] you can do nothing.**
> **6 If a person does not dwell in Me, he is thrown out like a [broken-off] branch, and withers; such branches are gathered up and thrown into the fire, and they are burned.**
> **7 If you live in Me [abide vitally united to Me] and My words remain in you and continue to live in your hearts, ask whatever you will, and it shall be done for you.**

Again and again, Jesus said, *"Dwell in Me... Abide in Me... Live in Me."* All three phrases, though using slightly different words, describe an intimately close connection with Christ that He longs to have with you. In a word: *fellowship*. Jesus wants vibrant, ongoing fellowship with you! That is what was lost in Eden, when Adam and Eve sinned, but it was restored through Christ's death, burial, and resurrection!

When we *dwell*, *abide*, and *live in fellowship* with Jesus, we receive a steady flow of all the spiritual nutrients we need to thrive and be productive. He is the Vine, and we are the branches. God designed us to live a fruitful, productive life, but bearing fruit is only possible when we dwell in Christ.

So, if you want to experience the "fruit" of His Spirit—things like love, joy, and peace—you must live *vitally united to Jesus*, the Vine. Again, this means spending time soaking in God's Word and communicating with Him in prayer. Time is the greatest building block of any relationship, and the more time you invest in praying as well as reading, studying, and meditating on the Word, the stronger your union with Him will be. It is truly amazing how peaceful life can be when you spend adequate time in the presence of God every day.

Marriage Is Like a Mirror
Reflecting Our Relationship with Jesus

What is interesting about the word *abide*, which is also translated as *dwell* in some Bible versions, is that in the original Greek text, it carries the idea of "staying in a state of expectancy." As we abide in fellowship with Christ, we have an expectancy or anticipation of hearing His voice, experiencing His love, and being in His presence.

In many ways, this is a picture of a healthy marriage in which the husband and wife have an expectancy or anticipation of being together, talking with one another, and receiving each other's love. The apostle Paul makes this comparison in Ephesians 5, comparing our relationship with Jesus like that of a husband and wife.

If you are married, hopefully you remember the expectancy you had when you were first dating and then preparing for marriage. My guess is that you couldn't wait to see each other the next time—to hold one another's hand, stare into each other's eyes, and be in one another's presence. Nothing was more important.

When my husband and I were dating, he traveled an hour and a half one way to bring me flowers and chocolates for Valentine's Day! Because of the distance, we usually only saw each other at church for services. But we both looked forward to those days with great anticipation because we really enjoyed spending time together.

In the same way, abiding vitally united to Jesus means we have a continual expectancy and an anticipation of spending time with Him. We can't wait to dive into His Word and hear Him speak new things to us that we have never seen before! We look forward to sitting in His presence, receiving His love, and loving Him back with our words of praise and worship. Nothing else compares to being together with Him.

The Lord Loves Us and Wants Us to Stay Red-Hot

Unfortunately, many believers get to a place where their expectancy and anticipation of spending time with Jesus fizzles out. When He gently knocks at the door of their heart, they ignore or dismiss His calls to spend time with Him.

That is exactly what happened to the believers at the church of Laodicea. Jesus was so grieved that their love for Him had grown cold that He dictated a letter to them through the apostle John.

> **REVELATION 3:15-16 (AMPC)**
> **15 I know your [record of] works and what you are doing; you are neither cold nor hot. Would that you were cold or hot!**
> **16 So, because you are lukewarm and neither cold nor hot, I will spew you out of My mouth!**

The Christians in Laodicea had become very prosperous and wealthy and felt that they were in need of nothing—not even the intimate fellowship of Jesus (see Revelation 3:17). Their indifference made the Lord sick to His stomach. Jealous for their affection, He corrected them, revealing to them their true condition and urging them to change their ways.

> **REVELATION 3:19 (MSG)**
> **The people I love, I call to account—prod and correct and guide so that they'll live at their best. Up on your feet, then! About face! Run after God!**

The believers in Laodicea weren't the only ones to lose their passion for Christ. Scripture tells us that the church of Ephesus had also "lost their first love." Passionately driven to regain first place in their lives, Jesus told them plainly,

REVELATION 2:4 (AMPC)
But I have this [one charge to make] against you: that you have left (abandoned) the love that you had at first [you have deserted Me, your first love].

How about you? Has your love for Jesus become lukewarm like the Laodiceans? Have you lost the passion you had for Him when you first got saved? If so, I believe Jesus is saying to you what He said to the believers at the church of Ephesus:

REVELATION 2:5 (AMPC)
Remember then from what heights you have fallen. Repent (change the inner man to meet God's will) and do the works you did previously [when first you knew the Lord], or else I will visit you and remove your lampstand from its place, unless you change your mind and repent.

Make no mistake—Jesus is still intensely in love with you! And He wants you to stay red-hot in love with Him. The very nature of the word *hot* carries the idea of a fiery, passionate pursuit of Him. He doesn't want to be second, third, or fourth—He wants to be *first*. He doesn't want the leftovers of your time—He wants the first fruits. Remember, He is your secret place.

Rather than abandon the love you first had for Jesus, He wants you to remember the things you did when you fell in love with Him and do those things again. That includes rekindling the excitement and expectancy of spending time with Him in His Word and in prayer. The more time you spend with Him, the more exciting your relationship will become. He will infuse you with His power, reveal His truth, and take you deeper into the Spirit than you've ever been before. When you're preoccupied with being in His Presence—the secret place—there is no room for thoughts of anxiety, worry, fear, or depression.

Jesus Spent Time in the Secret Place with the Father

Again, as believers, our secret place is *in Jesus*. In practical terms, time spent in His Word and praying in His presence is meant to be our continual dwelling place where we connect with Him intimately on a daily basis.

Jesus Himself gives us an example of what it looks like to passionately pursue time with the Father. Prophesying about Jesus, the prophet Isaiah said,

ISAIAH 50:4 (AMPC)
[The Servant of God says] The Lord God has given Me the tongue of a disciple and of one who is taught, that I should know how to speak a word in season to him who is weary. He wakens Me morning by morning, He wakens My ear to hear as a disciple [as one who is taught].

The "Servant of the Lord" Isaiah is talking about is *Jesus*. Therefore, it was Jesus who sought the Father "morning by morning," and the Father opened Jesus' ears and taught Him "how to speak a word in season" to every weary soul He encountered.

Jesus' practice of spending time in the secret place with the Father is confirmed in Mark 1:35 (NIV), which says, *"Very early in the morning, while it was still dark, Jesus got up, left the house and went off to a solitary place, where he prayed."* He also spent time with the Father in mountains, deserts, and gardens like Gethsemane (see Mark 6:46; Luke 5:16; John 18:1-2).

For us, meditating on the Word, and not just quickly reading it, will take us into the secret place with Jesus. Likewise, time spent in prayer—giving the Lord our undivided attention—will bring us into deeper intimacy with Him and the Father. This is especially true when we pray in the language of the Spirit (see Romans 8:26-27).

The Blessings of Abiding in the Secret Place

There are countless blessings available to us as we dwell in the secret place of Jesus Christ. Psalm 91 reveals many of them. Starting in verse 1 and going through verse 16, let's discover these benefits and learn what we need to do to experience them in our life.

PSALM 91:1 (AMPC)

The foundational verse says:

He who dwells in the secret place of the Most High shall remain stable and fixed under the shadow of the Almighty [Whose power no foe can withstand].

The word *dwells* in the original Hebrew means "to remain, to stay, or to settle." It can even be translated "to marry." As we noted, in a healthy marriage, a husband and wife spend quality time together whenever possible. As they *dwell* together, they talk, share things, and experience deep intimacy. Again, this reflects what our relationship with Jesus is to be like. Marriage gives us an understanding of the kind of intimacy the Lord is wanting with us.

In this place of intimacy—the secret place—we will remain *stable* and *fixed*. We won't be unstable or broken. There is no enemy or power that can withstand the power of Almighty God. In His presence, we are completely safe from anything with which the devil would try to attack us.

PSALM 91:2 (AMPC)

I will say of the Lord, He is my Refuge and my Fortress, my God; on Him I lean and rely, and in Him I [confidently] trust!

What is interesting about this verse is that in the original Hebrew text, the opening phrase actually says, *"I will say to the Lord."* This tells us that for us to benefit from the secret place and experience all the promises that come with this powerful position, we must first open our mouths and say something to God. Specifically, we must agree with God and say what He says. That is the instruction God Himself gives us in Isaiah 62:6 (AMPC), *"...put the Lord in remembrance [of His promises], keep not silence."*

In Psalm 91:2, the psalmist reminds the Lord that He is our Refuge and Fortress. Likewise, we need to open our mouth and say, "God is *my* Refuge and *my* Fortress, *my* God; on Him I lean and rely, and in Him I confidently trust!" This declaration gives us confidence and assurance of His care and provision.

PSALM 91:3 (AMPC)
For [then] He will deliver you from the snare of the fowler and from the deadly pestilence.

Notice the word *then.* When we are dwelling in the secret place and saying what God says, *then* we will be delivered from every *deadly* trap of Satan. That word *deadly* can also be translated *wicked* or *perverse.* It is through our declaration of faith that we will enjoy deliverance from every deadly and devastating thing, including disease. Thank God, that He delivers us from all of it!

PSALM 91:4 (AMPC)
[Then] He will cover you with His pinions, and under His wings shall you trust and find refuge; His truth and His faithfulness are a shield and a buckler.

God's truth is His Word. It is unchanging, absolute, and totally trustworthy, which is why we should put our faith in it. In Jeremiah 1:12 (AMPC), the Lord said, *"...I am alert and active, watching over My word to perform it."* When we trust in God's Word and His faithfulness, and speak His Word aloud, it acts as a shield to protect us.

> **PSALM 91:5-6 (AMPC)**
> **5 You shall not be afraid of the terror of the night, nor of the arrow (the evil plots and slanders of the wicked) that flies by day,**
> **6 Nor of the pestilence that stalks in darkness, nor of the destruction and sudden death that surprise and lay waste at noonday.**

When we are *dwelling* or *abiding* in the secret place and speaking God's promises aloud, we don't have to dread or fear anything—not even unseen terrors that come at night or piercing, surprise attacks that come in plain daylight.

I personalize this verse and say these words every day when I read this psalm. With bold faith, I declare, "I refuse to fear or dread anything, in Jesus' name! God has *not* given me a spirit of fear, but He has given me a spirit of *dunamis* power, *agape* love, and a sound, disciplined mind (see 2 Timothy 1:7)."

> **PSALM 91:7-8 (AMPC)**
> **7 A thousand may fall at your side, and ten thousand at your right hand, but it shall not come near you.**
> **8 Only a spectator shall you be [yourself inaccessible in the secret place of the Most High] as you witness the reward of the wicked.**

We see from this verse that even if thousands of people are falling away, failing, dying, or being overthrown, we will not be affected. Regardless of how many people have suffered a particular calamity, it will not be the standard for our lives.

I stood on this particular Scripture daily when I was recovering from anxiety. Medically speaking, I knew that many people who suffer from the kind of panic attack I was experiencing never completely recover from it because they always fear the next episode. Knowing this, I determined that I would not be one of those people. Even if 11,000 individuals have suffered from it, it would not be my destiny!

Furthermore, Psalm 91:8 tells us that when we dwell in the secret place, we are *inaccessible* to Satan. Jesus confirms this in John's gospel, telling us that no one can snatch us out of His hand or the Father's hand (see John 10:28-29). When we live in fellowship with Him, we are supernaturally protected and should never suffer the reward of the wicked.

PSALM 91:9-10 (AMPC)
9   Because you have made the Lord your refuge,
and the Most High your dwelling place,
10 There shall no evil befall you, nor any plague
or calamity come near your tent.

These two verses reiterate that action is required on our part. If we are going to experience God's protection, we must decide to purposely make the Lord Most High our dwelling place. When we do, God's Word says no evil will come near our dwelling.

PSALM 91:11-12 (AMPC)
11 For He will give His angels [especial] charge over you to accompany and defend and preserve you in all your ways [of obedience and service].
12 They shall bear you up on their hands, lest you dash your foot against a stone.

Here we see that the Lord has appointed His angels to guard and protect us in all our ways, which literally means "all the roads or courses our life takes." These angels are by our side and will watch us, save us, and preserve us. The phrase "bear you up on their hands" means they will "lift us up above all harm" and "carry us in the palm of their hands."

Keep in mind that for these angels to act, you must give them permission by agreeing with God. This requires you to open your mouth and say what His Word says: "God has given His angels [especial] charge over *me* to accompany and defend and preserve *me* in all *my* ways [of obedience and service]. They shall bear *me* up in their hands, lest *I* dash *my* foot against a stone."

The Bible teaches that angels are created to hearken unto the voice of the Lord and do His commandments (see Psalm 103:20). That means when we speak God's Word out loud, angels are listening and will swing into action to carry out what His Word says. Therefore, we must be careful to keep the Word in our hearts and in our mouths, so that we will always enjoy His angelic protection.

PSALM 91:13 (AMPC)

You shall tread upon the lion and adder; the young lion and the serpent shall you trample underfoot.

In the original Hebrew, the word *adder* refers to *a poisonous snake* like an asp, and the word *serpent* can also be translated as *dragon, sea monster,* or *whale.* Essentially, this verse is telling us that any life-threatening thing we encounter that seems larger than life, we will trample under our feet—it will not stop us from advancing into the plan of God for our life.

The New Testament counterpart to this verse is Luke 10:19-20, where Jesus said,

19 Behold, I give you the authority to trample on serpents and scorpions, and over all the power of the enemy, and nothing shall by any means hurt you.
20 Nevertheless do not rejoice in this, that the spirits are subject to you, but rather rejoice because your names are written in heaven.

It is so empowering to know that Jesus Himself has given us supernatural authority, and even ungodly spirits must obey us in His Name. The devil has absolutely no authority over us to steal, kill, or destroy. If we truly believe this and will declare with our mouth that we have authority over all the power of the enemy and that nothing shall by any means hurt us, we will never again have cause to fear anything.

PSALM 91:14 (AMPC)

Because he has set his love upon Me, therefore will I deliver him; I will set him on high, because he knows and understands My name [has a personal knowledge of My mercy, love, and kindness—trusts and relies on Me, knowing I will never forsake him, no, never].

Once again, we have a conditional promise: if we set our love upon God, He will deliver us. To "set our love upon Him" means we are desiring and longing for Him. That desire will cause us to make time for fellowship with Him. Quality time spent with Jesus in His Word and His presence will give us personal knowledge of His mercy, love, and kindness. The more we come to know Him, the more we will trust Him. Our Lord is the most faithful, reliable, and loving person in the world, and He always has our best interest at heart.

PSALM 91:15 (AMPC)

He shall call upon Me, and I will answer him; I will be with him in trouble, I will deliver him and honor him.

Wow! These are extraordinary promises! *"He shall call upon Me, and I will answer him..."* (Psalm 91:15). This verse lets us know that we can be confident that God will answer us because He hears us when we pray. How do we know for sure that He hears us when we cry out to Him? The answer is found here:

1 JOHN 5:14-15

14 Now this is the confidence that we have in Him, that if we ask anything according to His will, He hears us.
15 And if we know that He hears us, whatever we ask, we know that we have the petitions that we have asked of Him.

Any time we ask God for something according to His will—which is His Word—we can know with confidence that He heard us. And according to 1 John 5:15, if we know He heard us, we can know with absolute assurance that we have what we've asked for. The Amplified Classic translation says it this way:

1 JOHN 5:15 (AMPC)

And if (since) we [positively] know that He listens to us in whatever we ask, we also know [with settled and absolute knowledge] that we have [granted us as our present possessions] the requests made of Him.

Let's say we ask God for finances to pay for a need, or for a loved one to be delivered, it is His perfect will that we receive it. Likewise, if we ask for healing, including healing from anxiety or depression, it is God's will that we receive it. Once we pray and make our requests known to God, we should thank Him continually that what we've asked for is granted to us as our *present possession*. In other words, we should act like we already have it, and if we have it, we have no reason to worry or be depressed over it. How wonderful it is to belong to such a faithful God!

Looking back at Psalm 91:15, God also promises that He will be with us in trouble. Even when we face hard situations, the Lord is with us. Actually, that is what the name *Emmanuel* means, *God with us*. He promises to never leave us or forsake us (see Matthew 1:23; Hebrews 13:5).

He also promises to always deliver us out of trouble. We see this guarantee all through Scripture. Along with deliverance, God will also give us honor. Why? Because we have set our love on Him.

The final blessing listed for us who abide in the secret place is long life and salvation.

PSALM 91:16 AMPC
With long life will I satisfy him and show him My salvation.

If the devil is harassing you with thoughts that you will die young or not live your full life, know that he is a liar and there is no truth in him (see John 8:44). If you will stand on God's Word and declare that you will live a long life, you will win this mental battle.

I confess daily that God is giving me a long, satisfied life filled with His life, health, strength, wisdom, peace, joy, protection, and prosperity. I also declare that I am bearing much fruit (see John 15:8). A long life without these things is not a good life. If we plan to live long, then we must believe to finish strong.

God's perfect will for each of His children is to finish their race on earth with strength and with fruit that remains:

PSALM 92:12-15

12 The righteous shall flourish like a palm tree,
He shall grow like a cedar in Lebanon.
13 Those who are planted in the house of the
Lord shall flourish in the courts of our God.
14 They shall still bear fruit in old age; they
shall be fresh and flourishing,
15 To declare that the Lord is upright; He is my
rock, and there is no unrighteousness in Him.

If you are over 50 years old, you can still bear fruit. While many people plan to slow down and do less as they age, according to Psalm 92:14, the righteous will still be productive in old age. I plan to bear more fruit in the next twenty years than I did in the previous twenty years!

Some Closing Thoughts

As you can see, Psalm 91 is a psalm of promise, comfort, and victory. To receive these promises, you must abide in Christ—the secret place—and declare His Word out loud over your life and against the enemy.

The devil will not give you or anyone else a free pass. That is, he will not just leave you alone and let you effortlessly receive God's promises. A passive approach will not get the job done. On the contrary, you must fight the good fight of faith and take hold of these blessings to experience them in your life.

I encourage you to begin reading Psalm 91 every day and make it a personalized declaration you speak out loud to God and over your life. This is one thing I did that helped me overcome anxiety, and as I continue doing it daily, I continue to enjoy a peaceful mind and a fruitful life.

As you trust God for your complete freedom from anxiety, fear, and depression, make this psalm a part of your daily meditation and declaration. It is a great remedy for fear and will encourage you to remember that you can always depend on your heavenly Father to come through for you. As David said, you too will come to say: *"I sought the Lord, and he heard me, and delivered me from all my fears"* (Psalm 34:4).

MY PRAYER CONFESSION OF FAITH:

Lord, Your Word says that because I dwell in the secret place of the Most High, I remain stable in all my ways. I trust in You, Lord, and therefore, I am protected and delivered from every evil thing. You have given me authority over all the enemy's power and have assigned Your angels to watch over and protect me always. Thank You for giving me a long life that is satisfied with Your life, health, strength, wisdom, peace, joy, prosperity, and productivity. I praise You that I am bearing, and will continue to bear, much fruit all my days! In Your name, Jesus, Amen.

ADDITIONAL RESOURCES

Scriptures on God's Peace for Daily Meditation

"My son, give attention to my words; Incline your ear to my sayings. Do not let them depart from your eyes; keep them in the midst of your heart; for they are life to those who find them, And health to all their flesh."

— Proverbs 4:20-22

Nothing in this world compares to the priceless value of the Word of God. Proverbs 4:22 says the Word is *life* to us when we receive it and *health* to our flesh. The Hebrew word for *health* here describes *healing, soundness of mind,* or *a cure.* It carries the idea of "medicine" that restores our health. Just as many people take medication for mental health issues, according to this Scripture, God's Word is medicine to all our flesh. He is the Great Physician, and the medicine He prescribes is His Word. It will never expire or lose its potency.

God instructs us to take the medicine of His Word for everything that ails us—including anxiety and depression. The key to partaking of the life and healing energy in the Word is feeding on it until it penetrates our spirit. That is where it deposits supernatural life and healing.

Keep in mind that God's way of healing is spiritual. You take in—or feed on—His Word through hearing it, reading it, and pondering it in your mind. As you look at and attend to the Scriptures, meditating on and muttering them regularly, the Word penetrates your spirit and becomes a part of who you are. Its life-giving properties then go to work to bring health to every part of your being.

I have composed a list of Scriptures on the subject of peace for meditation. As you spend time reading these verses and their various translations out loud, the Word of God will penetrate your spirit and produce the desired result of peace. Remember to stay with it, and don't give up prematurely. Just as natural medicine often takes time to work in our bodies, it will likely take some time for the full effects of God's Word to kick in. Nevertheless, I believe you will find that God is truly faithful, and His Word will heal and deliver you as you spend time in it.

Psalm 4:8

NKJV—I will both lie down in peace, and sleep; for You alone, O Lord, make me dwell in safety.

AMPC—In peace I will both lie down and sleep, for You, Lord, alone make me dwell in safety and confident trust.

NLT—In peace I will lie down and sleep, for you alone, O Lord, will keep me safe.

MSG—At day's end I'm ready for sound sleep, for you, God, have put my life back together.

Psalm 29:11

NKJV—The Lord will give strength to His people; the Lord will bless His people with peace.

AMPC—The Lord will give [unyielding and impenetrable] strength to His people; the Lord will bless His people with peace.

Psalm 34:4

NKJV—I sought the Lord, and he heard me, and delivered me from all my fears.

AMPC—I sought (inquired of) the Lord and required Him [of necessity and on the authority of His Word], and He heard me, and delivered me from all my fears.

NLT—I prayed to the Lord, and he answered me. He freed me from all my fears.

Psalm 37:11

NKJV—But the meek shall inherit the earth, and shall delight themselves in the abundance of peace.

AMPC—But the humble will [at last] inherit the land and will delight themselves in abundant prosperity and peace.

Psalm 119:165

NKJV—Great peace have those who love Your law, and nothing causes them to stumble.

AMPC—Great peace have they who love Your law; nothing shall offend them or make them stumble.

NLT—Those who love your instructions have great peace and do not stumble.

Proverbs 3:1-2

NKJV—My son, do not forget my law, but let your heart keep my commands; for length of days and long life and peace they will add to you.

AMPC—My son, forget not my law or teaching, but let your heart keep my commandments; for length of days and years of a life [worth living] and tranquility [inward and outward and continuing through old age till death], these shall they add to you.

Isaiah 26:3-4

NKJV—You will keep him in perfect peace, whose mind is stayed on You, because he trusts in You. Trust in the Lord forever, for in Yah, the Lord, is everlasting strength.

AMPC—You will guard him and keep him in perfect and constant peace whose mind [both its inclination and its character] is stayed on You, because he commits himself to You, leans on You, and hopes confidently in You. So trust in the Lord (commit yourself to Him, lean on Him, hope confidently in Him) forever; for the Lord God is an everlasting Rock [the Rock of Ages].

NLT—You will keep in perfect peace all who trust in you, all whose thoughts are fixed on you! Trust in the Lord always, for the Lord God is the eternal Rock.

MSG—People with their minds set on you, you keep completely whole, steady on their feet, because they keep at it and don't quit. Depend on God and keep at it because in the Lord God you have a sure thing.

Isaiah 54:10

NKJV—"For the mountains shall depart and the hills be removed, but My kindness shall not depart from you, nor shall My covenant of peace be removed," says the Lord, who has mercy on you.

AMPC—For though the mountains should depart and the hills be shaken or removed, yet My love and kindness shall not depart from you, nor shall My covenant of peace and completeness be removed, says the Lord, Who has compassion on you.

MSG—"For even if the mountains walk away and the hills fall to pieces, my love won't walk away from you, my covenant commitment of peace won't fall apart." The God who has compassion on you says so.

Isaiah 54:13-14

NKJV—All your children shall be taught by the Lord, and great shall be the peace of your children. In righteousness you shall be established; you shall be far from oppression, for you shall not fear; and from terror, for it shall not come near you.

AMPC—And all your [spiritual] children shall be disciples [taught by the Lord and obedient to His will], and great shall be the peace and undisturbed composure of your children. You shall establish yourself in righteousness (rightness, in conformity with God's will and order): you shall be far from even the thought of oppression or destruction, for you shall not fear, and from terror, for it shall not come near you.

NLT—I will teach all your children, and they will enjoy great peace. You will be secure under a government that is just and fair. Your enemies will stay far away. You will live in peace, and terror will not come near.

Jeremiah 29:11

NKJV—For I know the thoughts that I think toward you, says the Lord, thoughts of peace and not of evil, to give you a future and a hope.

AMPC—For I know the thoughts and plans that I have for you, says the Lord, thoughts and plans for welfare and peace and not for evil, to give you hope in your final outcome.

NLT—"For I know the plans I have for you," says the Lord. "They are plans for good and not for disaster, to give you a future and a hope."

MSG—I know what I'm doing. I have it all planned out— plans to take care of you, not abandon you, plans to give you the future you hope for.

John 14:27

NKJV—Peace I leave with you, My peace I give to you; not as the world gives do I give to you. Let not your heart be troubled, neither let it be afraid.

AMPC—Peace I leave with you; My [own] peace I now give and bequeath to you. Not as the world gives do I give to you. Do not let your hearts be troubled, neither let them be afraid. [Stop allowing yourselves to be agitated and disturbed; and do not permit yourselves to be fearful and intimidated and cowardly and unsettled.]

NLT—I am leaving you with a gift—peace of mind and heart. And the peace I give is a gift the world cannot give. So don't be troubled or afraid.

MSG—I'm leaving you well and whole. That's my parting gift to you. Peace. I don't leave you the way you're used to being left—feeling abandoned, bereft. So don't be upset. Don't be distraught.

Romans 8:6

NKJV—For to be carnally minded is death, but to be spiritually minded is life and peace.

AMPC—Now the mind of the flesh [which is sense and reason without the Holy Spirit] is death [death that comprises all the miseries arising from sin, both here and hereafter]. But the mind of the [Holy] Spirit is life and [soul] peace [both now and forever].

NLT—So letting your sinful nature control your mind leads to death. But letting the Spirit control your mind leads to life and peace.

Romans 15:13

NKJV—Now may the God of hope fill you with all joy and peace in believing, that you may abound in hope by the power of the Holy Spirit.

AMPC—May the God of your hope so fill you with all joy and peace in believing [through the experience of your faith] that by the power of the Holy Spirit you may abound and be overflowing (bubbling over) with hope.

NLT—I pray that God, the source of hope, will fill you completely with joy and peace because you trust in him. Then you will overflow with confident hope through the power of the Holy Spirit.

Philippians 4:6-8

NKJV—Be anxious for nothing, but in everything by prayer and supplication, with thanksgiving, let your requests be made known to God; and the peace of God, which surpasses all understanding, will guard your hearts and minds through Christ Jesus. Finally, brethren, whatever things are true, whatever things are noble, whatever things are just, whatever things are pure, whatever things are lovely, whatever things are of good report, if there is any virtue and if there is anything praiseworthy—meditate on these things.

AMPC—Do not fret or have any anxiety about anything, but in every circumstance and in everything, by prayer and petition (definite requests), with thanksgiving, continue to make your wants known to God. And God's peace [shall be yours, that tranquil state of a soul assured of its salvation through Christ, and so fearing nothing from God and being content with its earthly lot of whatever sort that is, that peace] which transcends all understanding shall garrison and mount guard over your hearts and minds in Christ Jesus. For the rest, brethren, whatever is true, whatever is worthy of reverence and is honorable and seemly, whatever is just, whatever is pure, whatever is lovely and lovable, whatever is kind and winsome and gracious, if there is any virtue and excellence, if there is anything worthy of praise, think on and weigh and take account of these things [fix your minds on them].

NLT—Don't worry about anything; instead, pray about everything. Tell God what you need, and thank him for all he has done. Then you will experience God's peace, which exceeds anything we can understand. His peace will guard your hearts and minds as you live in Christ Jesus. And now, dear brothers and sisters, one final thing. Fix your thoughts on what is true, and honorable, and right, and pure, and lovely, and admirable. Think about things that are excellent and worthy of praise.

MSG—Don't fret or worry. Instead of worrying, pray. Let petitions and praises shape your worries into prayers, letting God know your concerns. Before you know it, a sense of God's wholeness, everything coming together for good, will come and settle you down. It's wonderful what happens when Christ displaces worry at the center of your life. Summing it all up, friends, I'd say you'll do best by filling your minds and meditating on things true, noble, reputable, authentic, compelling, gracious—the best, not the worst; the beautiful, not the ugly; things to praise, not things to curse.

Colossians 3:15

NKJV—And let the peace of God rule in your hearts, to which also you were called in one body; and be thankful.

AMPC—And let the peace (soul harmony which comes) from Christ rule (act as umpire continually) in your hearts [deciding and settling with finality all questions that arise in your minds, in that peaceful state] to which as [members of Christ's] one body you were also called [to live]. And be thankful (appreciative), [giving praise to God always].

NLT—And let the peace that comes from Christ rule in your hearts. For as members of one body you are called to live in peace. And always be thankful.

2 Thessalonians 3:16

NKJV—Now may the Lord of peace Himself give you peace always in every way. The Lord be with you all.

AMPC—Now may the Lord of peace Himself grant you His peace (the peace of His kingdom) at all times and in all ways [under all circumstances and conditions, whatever comes]. The Lord [be] with you all.

NLT—Now may the Lord of peace himself give you his peace at all times and in every situation. The Lord be with you all.

Psalm 23

NKJV—The Lord is my shepherd; I shall not want. He makes me to lie down in green pastures; He leads me beside the still waters. He restores my soul; He leads me in the paths of righteousness for His name's sake. Yea, though I walk through the valley of the shadow of death, I will fear no evil; for You are with me; Your rod and Your staff, they comfort me. You prepare a table before me in the presence of my enemies; You anoint my head with oil; my cup runs over. Surely goodness and mercy shall follow me all the days of my life; and I will dwell in the house of the Lord forever.

AMPC—The Lord is my Shepherd [to feed, guide, and shield me], I shall not lack. He makes me lie down in [fresh, tender] green pastures; He leads me beside the still and restful waters. He refreshes and restores my life (my self); He leads me in the paths of righteousness [uprightness and right standing with Him—not for my earning it, but] for His name's sake. Yes, though I walk through the [deep, sunless] valley of the shadow of death, I will fear or dread no evil, for You are with me; Your rod [to protect] and Your staff [to guide], they comfort me. You prepare a table before me in the presence of my enemies. You anoint my head with oil; my [brimming] cup runs over. Surely or only goodness, mercy, and unfailing love shall follow me all the days of my life, and through the length of my days the house of the Lord [and His presence] shall be my dwelling place.

NLT—The Lord is my shepherd; I have all that I need. He lets me rest in green meadows; he leads me beside peaceful streams. He renews my strength. He guides me along right paths, bringing honor to his name. Even when I walk through the darkest valley, I will not be afraid, for you are close beside me. Your rod and your staff protect and comfort me. You prepare a feast for me in the presence of my enemies. You honor me by anointing my head with oil. My cup overflows with blessings. Surely your goodness and unfailing love will pursue me all the days of my life, and I will live in the house of the Lord forever.

Psalm 91

I encourage you to read and meditate on Psalm 91 every day *(see Chapter 8)*. It is all about the blessings of abiding in the secret place!

The Most Important Step

I overcame anxiety through the supernatural help of the Lord Jesus Christ, and so can you. The starting place to receive God's help is making Jesus the Lord and Savior of your life. Once you take this life-changing step, you will receive all the help you need.

If you have not made Jesus your Lord and Savior, or you need to rededicate your life to Him, please take time right now to pray the prayer on the following page.

Prayer to Receive Jesus as Lord and Savior

Dear Heavenly Father,

I come to You in the name of Jesus. Your Word says, "…The one who comes to Me I will by no means cast out" (John 6:37). So, I know You won't reject me. You will take me in, and I thank You for it.

You said in Your Word, "…If you confess with your mouth the Lord Jesus and believe in your heart that God has raised Him from the dead, you will be saved…. For 'whoever calls on the name of the Lord shall be saved'" (Romans 10:9, 13).

Father, I believe in my heart that Jesus Christ is Your Son and that He died for my sins and was raised from the dead so I can be in right-standing with You. I am calling on His Name, the name of Jesus, so I know, Father, that You have saved me right now.

Your Word says, "…With the heart one believes unto righteousness, and with the mouth confession is made unto salvation" (Romans 10:10). I do believe with my heart, and I confess with my mouth that Jesus is my Lord. Therefore, I am saved! Thank You, Father.

If you prayed this prayer from your heart, you are a born-again child of God. Please contact us and let us know so that we can celebrate with you and send you some free materials to help you grow in your walk with God.

Please email us at hello@millerministries.org or write to:
Miller Ministries, 4000 Westbrook Dr, Aurora, IL 60504

You Tube

YouTube.com/MillerMinistries

About the Author

Christine Miller was raised in the Catholic faith and attended a Catholic elementary school. At the age of 16, she led worship for the guitar masses on Sundays. Although unusually committed to her church at a young age, Christine knew something was missing spiritually and always had a desire to know God better. It was in 1982, while attending college, that she received Jesus as her Lord and Savior. She went on to graduate from Evanston Hospital School of Nursing and later earned a bachelor's in theology from Life Christian University.

For the past 40 years, Christine has served full-time in ministry as an associate pastor, teacher, and administrator. She has helped her husband, Dr. Jeff Miller, pioneer three churches, including Abundant Life Family Church in Aurora, Illinois, where they currently pastor. Christine has a vibrant heart for missions, and has ministered in the Philippines and the Darién Jungle of Panama. She has conducted crusades, held alumni seminars, and preached in conferences and churches both locally and abroad.

The emphasis of her ministry centers on faith and healing. Christine operates in the word of knowledge, gifts of healings, and has an anointing to heal deaf ears. In addition to ministering weekly at Abundant Life Family Church, she hosts a YouTube program every Friday where she teaches people how to live victoriously.

Rev. Miller is ordained by World Harvest Church (Dufresne Ministries) and, along with her husband, is a member of Fresh Oil Fellowship Ministerial Association. Many value Christine's mentorship. If you would like to invite her to speak at your church or conference, please contact us at MillerMinistries.org.